One Step at a Time

BUILDING A BETTER MARRIAGE, FAMILY, AND YOU

Joe J. Christensen

Deseret Book
Salt Lake City, Utah

To my wife, Barbara, our children and their spouses,
and our grandchildren—with undying love and appreciation

Library of Congress Cataloging-in-Publication Data

Christensen, Joe J.
   One step at a time : building a better marriage, family, and you / by Joe J. Christensen.
      p.   cm.
   Includes index.
   ISBN 1-57345-188-6
   1. Marriage—Religious aspects—Church of Jesus Christ of Latter-day Saints. 2. Church of Jesus Christ of Latter-day Saints—Membership. 3. Mormon Church—Membership. 4. Family—Religious life. 5. Christian life—Mormon authors. I. Title.
BX8641.C48   1996
248.4'89332—dc20   96-16342
                                           CIP

Printed in the United States of America

10 9 8 7 6 5 4 3 2 1

Contents

Acknowledgments

The idea for writing some suggestions for strengthening marriage and family came to me years ago as I hoped that I might share something that would be of help to our own children and grandchildren. Since the conception of that idea, the period of gestation has been a long one.

I appreciate the encouragement of Sheri Dew and Ron Millett, from the administration of Deseret Book Company, who were responsible for motivating me to take the major leap of getting pen to paper and fingers to keyboard. I am grateful to the entire editing and production staff at Deseret Book, who have been most helpful and professional in this entire detailed process. I am particularly indebted to Emily Watts for her careful and insightful work in editing the original manuscript.

Some of the resource materials for this book came from efforts I had made earlier in the preparation of speeches and other regular assignments associated with my calling. In this effort I was greatly helped by my secretary, Geneene Brady, who patiently tolerated what I am sure seemed to her to be an endless series of drafts of presentations. In early mornings and late evenings, I drew on those materials.

In addition, I must express appreciation to my wife, Barbara, and our children for their valued comments and suggestions. No group can be more candid—and consequently of more real help—than one's own family. Most of all, I am grateful for their lives and association, which provided me with so many instructive family examples.

In the text—to protect their privacy—I have taken the liberty of changing the names of some of the individuals whose examples I cite.

Although I have made a conscientious effort to keep the message of the book consistent with the doctrine and teachings of The Church of Jesus Christ of Latter-day Saints, it needs to be understood that this is not an official Church publication. I take full personal responsibility for its content.

If only a few readers find in this modest effort something of value that will strengthen their marriages, their families, and themselves, I will have been well recompensed for the effort.

Introduction

Perhaps you remember the comedian who said, "I took a course in speed-reading, learning to read straight down the middle of the page, and I was able to go through Tolstoy's *War and Peace* in twenty minutes. . . . It's about Russia."

This little volume was not meant to be speed-read. As you go through it, you will benefit most if you take the time to read and then analyze yourself carefully. See which suggestions might best help you to improve your marriage, your family, or yourself. We all have plenty of room for improvement, and we all need to progress in a variety of ways. As I write these ideas I certainly don't feel that I have "arrived"; I recognize that there is much for us all to do to improve.

The book is organized into three parts and can be read in any order that seems to fit your needs at the moment. The three areas of marriage, family, and self are all intertwined, and improving in one area will likely help you move forward in the others as well.

Years ago, an influential professor gave me some good advice. He said, "Joe, remember that you will never be a better husband, father, or teacher than you are a person. If you work to improve yourself, most other things will fall into place in your life. I'm pleased that you are going to work on some graduate degrees. I'd suggest that when you finish and you receive that diploma, put it in a drawer and forget about it. Just do the job, whatever it is, to the best of your ability and be your best self."

This book is about "being your best self," about becoming a better person, a better spouse, a better parent. If you will take the time for careful study, self-analysis, prayer, and resolution, you can make corrections that will enrich your life and enhance your possibilities.

PART ONE

Building a Better Marriage

I wish you could have known my parents. By nature, Dad was somewhat shy. He was not the type to seek opportunities for speaking in public, even though he served as bishop of our little ward in Banida, Idaho, for nine years. He was a man of few words. My mother, on the other hand, was much more outgoing. I don't think she had ever met a "stranger" in her life. She liked to socialize, and she communicated her interest in and love for people quite naturally. Their marriage was an interesting blend of complementary personalities. It was fascinating to observe them.

Mom passed away in 1976, and Dad spent the next nine lonely years as a widower before he also passed away. A few months after my mother died, I was traveling on a work assignment in the area of our old family home, and I stopped in unannounced to see how Dad was doing.

As usual, I entered without knocking. I found Dad seated alone at the kitchen table. He seemed embarrassed that I would see him with tears running down his cheeks. He wiped them away with the back of his hand and said, "Son, I was just sitting here wondering why your mother had to leave me so soon." "So soon"—even though they had celebrated their golden wedding anniversary not long before. Fifty years together was definitely not long enough! That is the nature of true love.

Earlier, at Mom's urging, Dad had written his personal history. The entire document filled *part* of one page. (I told you he was a man of few words!) Among those few words are these, which for us have come to be like family scripture: "After forty-four years of married life, she is still the most wonderful woman I have ever known." We knew that Mom and Dad loved each other, yet it is special for us to have those words written by his own hand.

Someone once said, "The greatest gift a father can give to his children is to love their mother." Dad gave us that gift, and for it we will be eternally grateful.

As I look back now on my parents' marriage, as solid and enduring as it was, I am sure that it could have been better in a variety of ways. That's true of every marriage, isn't it? Regardless of how good a marriage may be, it could be better.

The following ideas suggest different areas you might focus on to strengthen your marriage. You might profit most by reading them together with your spouse and working on them as a couple. If you consider these recommendations in an open, honest, and caring way, you can experience the joy of seeing your marriage blossom. What could be of more importance to you and your family?

Remember the Central Importance of Marriage and Family

From the day the Church was organized in 1830 to the present, only five proclamations have been issued to the world from the First Presidency and the Quorum of the Twelve. The first four occurred in the years 1841, 1845, 1865, and 1980. On September 25, 1995, at the general Relief Society meeting, President Gordon B. Hinckley read the most recent proclamation, the subject of which is the family.

The Proclamation on the Family begins: "We, the First Presidency and the Council of the Twelve Apostles of The Church of Jesus Christ of Latter-day Saints, solemnly proclaim that marriage between a man and a woman is ordained of God and that the family is central to the Creator's plan for the eternal destiny of His children." The Church of Jesus Christ stands as firm as the Rock of Gibraltar on issues related to marriage and the family, in spite of the unsettling currents and shifting sands of our modern society. As stated in the proclamation, "The family is ordained of God. Marriage between man and woman is essential to His eternal plan. Children are entitled to birth within the bonds of matrimony, and to be reared by a father and a mother who honor marital vows with complete fidelity. Happiness in family life is most likely to be achieved when founded upon the teachings of the Lord Jesus Christ. Successful marriages and families are established and maintained on principles of faith, prayer, repentance, forgiveness, respect, love, compassion, work, and wholesome recreational activities."

I have never met anyone who did not want to make a success of his or her marriage. It doesn't matter what the circumstances are surrounding the union, everyone is inclined to hope that the lyrics of the love song will become a reality for them: "I'll be loving you always." We never hear people say, "Sweetheart, let's hurry up and get married so we can get divorce proceedings started more quickly." No one marries hoping for divorce, but the sad reality is that an increasing number of marriages are ending in separation, sadness, and divorce—with a good share of the divorces occurring within the first five years.

Nothing could be more important to our happiness than establishing a sound marriage. Contemplate these words from Elder Bruce R. McConkie:

> From the moment of birth into mortality to the time we are married in the temple, everything we have in the whole gospel system is to prepare and qualify us to enter that holy order of matrimony which makes us husband and wife in this life and in the world to come.
>
> Then from the moment we are sealed together by the power and authority of the holy priesthood . . . everything connected with revealed religion is designed to help us keep the terms and conditions of our marriage covenant, so that this covenant will have . . . force in the life to come.
>
> Thus celestial marriage is the crowning ordinance of the gospel, the . . . most important organization in time or in eternity. . . . We should have more interest

in and concern for our families than for anything else in life. . . .

There is nothing in this world as important as the creation and perfection of family units. (*Improvement Era,* June 1970, pp. 43–44)

Without doubt, these words are true. They support what we read in scriptures and in statements from modern prophets. If we look back to the beginning of time, we recognize that marriage was apparently one of the prime reasons for the creation and placement of men and women on this earth. After the creation of Eve, Adam said, "This is now bone of my bones, and flesh of my flesh. . . . Therefore shall a man leave his father and his mother, and shall cleave unto his wife: and they shall be one flesh" (Genesis 2:23–24). The Doctrine and Covenants stresses this responsibility of establishing enduring marriages even more specifically: "Thou shalt love thy wife with all thy heart, and shalt cleave unto her and *none else*" (D&C 42:22; emphasis added).

A major hope and goal of all who marry is to find happiness—but no one claims that achieving an excellent, happy marriage is an easy process. That goal of happiness is not accomplished without some genuine effort on the part of each spouse. Elder Dean L. Larsen has said: "Marriage is not an easy venture. It is largely a one-time-through, do-it-yourself project for the husband and wife. I repeatedly encounter the illusion today, especially among younger people, that perfect marriages happen simply if the right two people come together. This is untrue. Marriages don't succeed automatically. Those who build happy, secure, successful marriages pay the price to do so. They work at it constantly" (*Ensign,* March 1985, p. 20).

We can't expect a successful marriage to be achieved without some solid, mature efforts. A *Deseret News* editorial stated: "There seems to be a superstition among many thousands of our young who hold hands and smooch in the drive-ins that marriage is a cottage surrounded by perpetual hollyhocks to which a perpetually young and handsome husband comes home to a perpetually young and ravishing wife. When the hollyhocks wither and boredom and bills appear the divorce courts are jammed. . . . Anyone who imagines that bliss is normal is going to waste a lot of time running around and shouting that he has been robbed" (*Deseret News,* June 12, 1973, p. A4).

When two people have made sacred marital promises to each other and have faithfully kept them, they are in a position to face whatever challenges life may offer. To illustrate, Elder Marlin K. Jensen described a moving situation:

> Recently, I visited with a widower as he stood bravely at the side of his wife's casket, surrounded by several handsome and stalwart sons. This man and his wife had been married for fifty-three years, during the last six of which she had been seriously ill with a terminal kidney disease. He had provided the 24-hour care she required until his own health was in jeopardy. I expressed my admiration for him and the great love and care he had given his wife. I felt compelled to ask, "How did you do it?"
>
> It was easy, he replied, when he remembered that fifty-three years earlier, he had knelt at an altar in the temple and made a covenant with the Lord and with his bride. "I wanted to keep it," he said.
>
> In an eternal marriage, the thought of ending what began with a covenant between God and each other simply has little place. When challenges come and our individual weaknesses are revealed, the remedy is to repent, improve, and apologize, not to separate or divorce. When we make covenants with the Lord and our eternal companion, we should do everything in our power to honor the terms. (*Ensign,* October 1994, p. 51)

That feeling is consistent with what Paul wrote to the Corinthian Saints, "Neither is the man without the woman, neither the woman without the man, in the Lord" (1 Corinthians 11:11). Emphasizing that point, President Joseph F. Smith declared: "No man can be saved and exalted in the kingdom of God without the woman, and no woman can reach perfection and exaltation in the kingdom of God, alone. . . . One is not perfect without the other" (in Conference Report, April 1913, p. 118).

We live in a time when many do not feel that being formally married is necessary at all. Witness the number of couples who simply decide to live together without the benefit of the enduring covenants and promises of marriage that could help make their relationship more lasting and meaningful. There are also a few who make vows of celibacy. The Lord made it clear that marriage is important when he said, "And again, verily I say unto you, that whoso forbiddeth to marry is not ordained of God, for marriage is ordained of God unto man" (D&C 49:15).

Even though marriage is ordained of God, there are those who will not marry in this life. President Hinckley has reiterated a special promise made by a variety of prior prophets to those who remain single through no choice of their own, and also a caution to those who could marry and choose not to: "My heart reaches out to those among us, especially our single sisters, who long for marriage and cannot seem to find it. Our Father in Heaven reserves for them every promised blessing. I have far less sympathy for the young men, who under the customs of our society, have the prerogative to take the initiative in these matters but in so many cases fail to do so. Strong words have been spoken to them in the past by Presidents of this church" (*Ensign,* May 1991, p. 71).

Considering the importance of marriage in this life as well as in the hereafter, a couple would be wise not even to entertain the idea of divorce except in the most extreme circumstances. We must exert our every energy to avoid it. President Spencer W. Kimball said: "It has come to be a common thing to talk about divorce. The minute there is a little crisis or a little argument in the family, we talk about divorce, and we rush to see an attorney. This is not the way of the Lord. We should go back and adjust our problems and make our marriage compatible and sweet and blessed" (*Marriage and Divorce* [Salt Lake City: Deseret Book, 1976], pp. 30–31).

Not long ago, a friend of mine who is serving as a stake president invited all the bishops in his stake to list what they thought was the greatest problem leading to divorce among the members of their wards. The most common problem listed was selfishness. President Hinckley agreed that selfishness was the root cause of the increasing number of broken homes.

If we are having marital difficulties, we need to analyze ourselves. To what degree are we letting our own selfishness stand in the way of a good marriage? Consider these wise observations:

> Selfishness so often is the basis of money problems, which are a very serious and real factor affecting the stability of family life. Selfishness is at the root of adultery, the breaking of solemn and sacred covenants to satisfy selfish lust. Selfishness is the antithesis of love. It is a cankering expression of greed. It destroys self-discipline. It obliterates loyalty. It tears up sacred covenants. It afflicts both men and women. Sometimes we allow our jobs or professions to come before our spouses. We sometimes allow our children, or our Church callings, our recreational pursuits, to come before our spouses. ("Strengthening a Marriage," *Church News*, July 7, 1990, p. 16)

President Hinckley has described much of what leads to divorce: "Too many who come to marriage have been coddled and spoiled and somehow led to feel that everything must be precisely right at all times, that life is a series of entertainments, that appetites are to be satisfied without regard to principle. How tragic the consequences of such hollow and unreasonable thinking!" (*Ensign*, May 1991, p. 73).

Granted, there are occasions when divorce is the only viable option, but it should be very rare. What are the grounds that justify divorce? President James E. Faust has said:

> Marriage between man and woman is a natural state and is ordained of God. It is a moral imperative. Those marriages performed in our temples, meant to be eternal relationships, then, become the most sacred covenants we can make. The sealing power given by God through Elijah is thus invoked, and God becomes a party to the promises. . . .
>
> In my opinion, "just cause" should be nothing less serious than a prolonged and apparently irredeemable relationship which is destructive of a person's dignity as a human being.
>
> At the same time, I have strong feelings about what is not provocation for breaking the sacred covenants of marriage. Surely it is not simply "mental distress," nor "personality differences," nor "having grown apart," nor having "fallen out of love." (*Ensign*, May 1993, pp. 36–37)

Not long ago I had a conversation with a man sitting next to me on a flight to Los Angeles. I learned that he was a certified public accountant on his way to Acapulco for a week of relaxation following his tax season of work. Since he was alone, I asked him if any other members of his family were going to be there with him. "No, I'm going alone," he replied. "You see, my wife and I are now separated. After thirty years of marriage and with our three children married, I decided that I would move out. We had grown apart."

I asked, "What do you feel was the biggest problem?"

"Really, it was my fault," he answered. "You see, I'm a workaholic. I found that I would work seven days a week. I would leave home before the children were out of bed and return after they were asleep. We really didn't have much of an association. In a way, I was married to my work. I saw that there was always plenty of money, including educational trust funds for the children, cars, medical support, and so on. It shocked me one evening when I did happen to come home a little early and discover that my daughter was dressed to go to a prom. Here she was seventeen. Where had all the years gone? It seemed to me that she should still be only about twelve or thirteen. I just grew away. My wife was willing to go 110 percent and I guess I was only willing to go about 10 or 20 percent. My work almost became my life and, as a result, I sacrificed my marriage and my family. Really, I am to blame more than anyone else."

I encouraged him to give some serious thought to studying the gospel and letting the influence of the Spirit and of righteous living help to heal him and his marriage. I invited him to bring his family together—for time and all eternity. When he left, he said that he would give the idea of getting back together with his wife some serious thought as he was lying out on the beach during his week in Acapulco.

Frequently, and I think it is the situation in the case just cited, couples who choose to divorce have solvable problems. If only they realized that, rather than being an easy out or an escape, divorce often means moving from a bad situation to a worse one. Dr. Victor Cline quoted from a divorced husband the following observation: "If I had known what lay ahead after the divorce, I know I would have put more effort into trying to save my marriage and resolving our differences. That might have been possible, because my wife did have a number of very positive qualities. My problem was that I was very stubborn; it was a matter of pride for me" (*Ensign,* July 1993, p. 17).

After contemplating many couples' problems, a professional marriage counselor said, "I could not think of one case of divorce where the couple had been treating each other kindly." I agree with President Hinckley's observation that "a happy marriage is not so much a matter of romance as it is an anxious concern for the comfort and well-being of one's companion."

President George Q. Cannon made this significant statement about the importance of marriage and the growing possibilities of love throughout the eternities:

> We believe that when a man and woman are united as husband and wife, and they love each other, their hearts and feelings are one, that that love is as enduring as eternity itself, and that when death overtakes them it will *neither extinguish nor cool that love, but that it will brighten and kindle it to a purer flame,* and that it will endure through eternity; and that if we have offspring they will be with us and our mutual associations will be one of the chief joys of the heaven to which we are hastening. . . . God has restored the everlasting priesthood, by which ties can be formed, . . . which shall be as enduring as we ourselves are enduring, . . . and they and their children will dwell and associate together eternally, and this, as I have said, will *constitute one of the chief joys of heaven; and we look forward to it with delightful anticipations. (Journal of Discourses,* 26 vols. [Liverpool: Latter-day Saints Book Depot, 1855–86], 14:320–21; emphasis added)

Marriage is vitally important. It was ordained by God and intended to be sealed forever. We should do all in our power to preserve our marriages. We should follow the counsel to overcome selfishness and do everything we can to seek the comfort and happiness of our mates. I like the suggestion that if you really want to know the nature of the person you married, read your spouse's patriarchal blessing, and you will come to know that you have married one of our Heavenly Father's choicest sons or daughters. If you will do everything you can to help him or her achieve the maximum possible development in this mortal life, you will thus contribute to the Father's great plan of happiness.

IDEA 2

Make the Lord a Partner in Your Marriage

Years ago, when it was common for a General Authority on a mission tour to interview all the missionaries, Elder Spencer W. Kimball was visiting with a young elder who was near the end of his mission.

"When you get released, Elder, what are your plans?"

"Oh, I plan to go back to college," he said, and added, smiling, "and then I hope to fall in love and get married."

The apostle shared this counsel: "Well, don't just pray to marry the one you love. Pray to love the one you marry."

This is very important counsel: Pray, literally pray—in your private prayers and in those with your mate—that your love for each other will increase as time goes on. There is no mutual objective of greater importance for you, your marriage, or your posterity.

Many Church leaders as well as professional counselors have indicated that they have never seen a marriage in serious difficulty in which the couple was still praying together daily. When you invite the Lord to be a partner in your union, there is a softening of feelings, a moderation of tension that occurs through the power of the Spirit. See what happens when, as you kneel together, you hear your companion express gratitude and love for you.

Pray that you, working together, may overcome whatever difficulties you may have so that your love can increase.

When differences do arise, few things can be more helpful than praying together. It is hard for me to hold onto any negative feelings after I have heard Barbara include such sincere expressions in her prayers as, "Father, we are so grateful to have found each other. Wilt Thou bless us and forgive us when we say or do anything that would weaken the love we have for each other."

Sometimes, when Barbara has not been feeling well or has been discouraged for whatever reason, it has seemed to me to be helpful and meaningful during our joint companion prayer to shift into the first person and genuinely express my feelings, "Father, I am so grateful to have a companion such as Barbara. Help her to know how much I love and appreciate her as one of Thy chosen daughters. Assist her to be healed completely and given the health and strength she needs to continue on with her life's important mission as wife and mother."

A young wife and mother of four mentioned how much strength she had received from one verse in the Book of Mormon. She felt that it had helped her personally to overcome problems and weaknesses, and that her husband had benefited from it as well. Ether 12:27 is brightly marked in her own copy of the scriptures:

"And if men come unto me I will show unto them their weakness. I give unto men weakness that they may be humble; and my grace is sufficient for all men that humble themselves before me; for if they humble themselves before me, and have faith in me, then will I make weak things become strong unto them." As we humble ourselves and seek the Lord's grace, we can receive an added measure of strength for our challenges.

I would invite you to candidly analyze your situation. Are you and your companion praying together daily that your marriage may be strengthened? If not, now is an excellent time to start!

IDEA 3

Learn to Listen

In the Epistle of James we read some very good advice: "Let every man be swift to hear, slow to speak, slow to wrath" (James 1:19). Dr. Brent Barlow shared this experience: "Not long ago I was invited to teach a priesthood lesson in our ward on husband-wife relationships. During the lesson, I asked the quorum members how many would like to receive a revelation. Every hand went up. I then suggested that we all go home and ask our wives how we could be better husbands. (I should add that I followed my own advice, and had a very informative discussion with [my wife] Susan for more than an hour that afternoon!)" (*Ensign,* September 1992, p. 17). We need to listen.

Have you ever had your spouse say something like I heard not long ago, "Joe, are you listening?" Barbara is not the only one who is concerned about my listening. Some time ago, I was taking a nap and our little grand-daughter Allison came and lifted up one of my eyelids and said, "Grandpa, are you in there?" We should be "in there" and always responsive to our companions.

"He that hath ears to hear, let him hear" (Matthew 11:15).

Becoming a good listener requires practice and concentration. It takes genuine effort to listen. It is estimated that ordinary conversation moves at a rate of about 125 words per minute and that we think at about 400 words per minute, so it is possible for our minds to wander or be on other things while someone is speaking to us. Author Margaret Lane wrote: "A hostess once decided to test how well people listen. Serving canapés, she remarked, 'Do try one. I've filled them with strychnine.' Not a single guest hesitated. 'Lovely,' they said, 'I must have your recipe'" ("Are You Really Listening?" *Reader's Digest,* November 1980, p. 183).

Some specific suggestions can help us become better listeners: Maintain eye contact. Avoid attempting to do something else, such as watching television, while you listen. Nod your head in an encouraging way. Be sure to avoid tapping your foot or looking at your watch, thus communicating that you really don't have the time or the desire to listen. A husband especially should remember that in many cases his wife has been at home caring for the children and may not have had the opportunity for an adult conversation all day. She really needs someone who will listen attentively.

Sometimes we fail as listeners because we feel that we have to make a comment on every subject. A leading communications expert, Dr. S. I. Hayakawa, observed:

> Listening does not mean simply maintaining a polite silence while you are rehearsing in your mind the speech you are going to make the next time you can grab a conversational opening.
>
> Nor does listening mean waiting alertly for the flaws in the other fellow's arguments so that later you can mow him down. Listening means trying to see the problem the way the speaker sees it—which means not sympathy, which is feeling for him, but empathy, which is experiencing with him. Listening requires entering actively and imaginatively into the other fellow's situation and trying to understand a frame of reference different from your own (*The Use and Misuse of*

Language [Greenwich, Conn.: Fawcett Publishing, 1943], p. 73).

All of us hunger to be heard. Doctors' and counselors' offices are filled with people whose main need is to have someone listen to them. An unknown author has written: "His thoughts were slow, his words were few, and never formed to glisten, but he was a joy to all his friends—You should have heard him listen."

Sometimes when we don't listen, differences and even quarrels can develop. We proceed without being as sensitive as we should be to our companions' feelings. One or the other may become offended and cut off communication. There may be times when it is wiser to "let the sun go down on your wrath" and wait until sufficient time has passed so that you can return to a problem more rested and calm. But the time for listening must come, or the "silent treatment" can result, which in extreme cases can go on for hours, days, or even months. With one couple, communication had broken down to the incredible point that they never communicated directly with each other but rather had one of their children or the husband's students take messages back and forth.

In order to help keep channels open, here are some practical hints adapted from counsel given by Dr. Edwin G. Brown, former dean of graduate social work at the University of Utah. The suggestions can help couples improve communication with each other in a crisis:

1. Share! Talk about what you are feeling, experiencing, and understanding about each other.

2. Be yourself. Share your thoughts and feelings openly, naturally.

3. Get into the specifics. Talk in detail about what is going on between you.

4. Listen. How do you "come across" to the other person—how do you affect him or her?

5. Accept what you hear. By learning what the other person is thinking, feeling, and wanting, you can decide what he or she needs and how you fit into the picture.

6. Tune in on those inner promptings of love and compassion.

7. Act in accordance with your instincts and insights you are acquiring from shared experiences and feelings.

There is no one to whom we should give more undivided listening attention than our spouses. They know us better than anyone and are in the best position to give us suggestions for improving ourselves or our relationships. We should remember that we really need to improve—as someone has said, "Repentance is a full-time job for all mortals." Whatever your situation, resolve to be a good listener and your marriage will be strengthened.

Avoid "Ceaseless Pinpricking"

Barbara and I had a personal visit with President Spencer W. Kimball at the time that we were married. He gave us some wonderful counsel: "Don't ever be critical of each other, even in jest. Never run each other down—especially in the presence of others—because sooner or later one of you will get your feelings hurt and it won't be a joke anymore. Always build each other. Compliment each other in the presence of your friends and you will reap great rewards in your companionship."

As a result of that counsel, we have noticed when we have been with people who have criticized each other that, in several instances, their relationship was not as strong and positive as it ought to have been.

Constant criticism, or "ceaseless pinpricking," as President Kimball called it, can deflate any marriage (see *Marriage and Divorce* [Salt Lake City: Deseret Book, 1976], p. 19). We should not be too critical of each other's faults. There has been only one perfect person on this earth, and we all know who He was. That means that we have all married imperfect people. We should always understand that our mate is not perfect. Of even more importance, though it may be hard for some to accept, we should remember that our mate's mate is not perfect either. We all have a long way to go in developing Christlike qualities.

Rather than criticize, we should apply the principles of Johnny Lingo's "eight-cow wife," illustrated by an experience my wife, Barbara, had while we were serving at the Missionary Training Center. She remembers it this way:

> We had a fine couple who came through the MTC while we were there. One day their instructor came in and asked if I would talk with them. He said that he had some concern for them—especially the wife. He explained to me that she didn't learn the scripture memorization quite as quickly as her husband did and that the husband would show his disapproval in the class and then she would get more flustered than ever. (There were just the two of them in the class with the teacher.) The teacher said that the wife was having a great deal of trouble with hives, and he wondered if it could possibly be related to the stress in the class. That afternoon the couple stopped by my office.
>
> After they had seated themselves in my office, I began to visit with them and told the wife how sorry I was that she was being plagued with the hives. I asked how long she had had them. (She was looking down at her hands in her lap as they twirled a handkerchief around and around.) Her husband answered: "She's had them several times." "Have you seen a doctor?" I asked her. More twirling. He quickly said, "I've taken her to doctors and there is nothing wrong with her."
>
> I think by then I was getting the picture and so I said to him, "Elder So-and-So, Heavenly Father has blessed all of us with gifts and talents. Apparently, you have a fine talent for memorizing scriptures and other things. I am sure you are grateful for that. It is to be admired. Your wife has talents that you do not have. Somehow, Heavenly Father seems to balance them out in each of us." I then suggested to him that one of the

main callings we have in a marriage is to build each other and increase the self-image and esteem of our partners. I told him the story of Johnny Lingo (one of my favorites). I told him about President Gunther of the Provo Temple, how his wife would have to leave early some mornings for her duties at the temple. On those mornings she would leave a glass of freshly squeezed orange juice for him on the table because she knew it was such a favorite. She would tuck a note underneath the glass saying something like: "Lucky Provo Temple to have you for its president. You're the greatest!"

I mentioned to them (particularly to him) about our children's observing Elder Russell M. Nelson, before he became a General Authority, helping his wife tenderly into the car and offering other nice considerations. We talked about another missionary couple who had come through the MTC some time before. We had known them and were glad to see and visit with them. As they conversed with us, she corrected everything he said. According to her, he didn't quite make one correct statement all the time they visited with us. I paraphrased Goethe, "Treat a person as he is and he will stay as he is. However, treat him as if he could become someone great and outstanding and he will become exactly that." Criticism will have the opposite effect. I finished by quoting from a scene in *My Fair Lady* when Eliza was talking to Colonel Pickering. She said, "To Professor Higgins, I will always be a flower girl. But, to you, I can become a queen, because you treat me like a queen."

I really gathered my courage and said to the husband, "How long has it been since you have complimented this lovely lady on something she has done and been loving to her?" And they left my office.

Two days later they returned. When I answered their knock at the door, he began by saying, "Well, we have just wasted two months!" They came in and sat down and then, much to my surprise, he began crying. He said to me, "Can you believe that I have been doing that to her for forty years?" They had obviously had quite a visit for the two days they had been gone from my office. He had completed the most difficult exercise of all—that of looking in the mirror and asking, "Am I to blame?"

I noticed that she sat in her chair this time looking up all the while. She was not toying with her handkerchief. I was overjoyed by the expression on her face and how happy she looked. They left the next day hand in hand for the airport after they stopped in to say good-bye. They had a new relationship after forty years. If we desire to have an eight-cow marriage partner or a two-cow one, it is up to us. We need to build them each day and let them know we think they are truly "eight-cow" people.

There is great meaning in the statement by Robert Bierstedt: "It isn't what *I* think of me, and it isn't what *you* think of me, but it is what I *think* you think of me." We tend to be painfully aware of our weaknesses—most of us don't need frequent reminders. Few people have ever changed for the better as a result of constant nagging. If we are not careful, some of what we offer as constructive criticism is actually destructive.

At times, it is better to leave some things unsaid. One woman described an experience she had early in her marriage:

> My husband and I had been married about two years—just long enough for me to realize that he was a normal man rather than a knight on a white charger— when I read a magazine article recommending that married couples schedule regular talks to discuss, truthfully and candidly, the habits or mannerisms they find annoying in each other. The theory was that if the partners knew of such annoyances, they could correct them before resentful feelings developed.

It made sense to me. I talked with my husband about the idea. After some hesitation, he agreed to give it a try.

As I recall, we were to name five things we found annoying, and I started off. After more than fifty years, I remember only my first complaint: grapefruit. I told him that I didn't like the way he ate grapefruit. He peeled it and ate it like an orange! Nobody else I knew ate grapefruit like that. Could a girl be expected to spend a lifetime, and even eternity, watching her husband eat grapefruit like an orange? Although I have forgotten them, I'm sure the rest of my complaints were similar.

After I finished, it was his turn to tell the things he disliked about me. Though it has been more than half a century, I still carry a mental image of my husband's handsome young face as he gathered his brows together in a thoughtful, puzzled frown and then looked at me with his large blue-gray eyes and said, "Well, to tell the truth, I can't think of anything I don't like about you, Honey."

Gasp.

I quickly turned my back, because I didn't know how to explain the tears that had filled my eyes and were running down my face. I had found fault with him over such trivial things as the way he ate grapefruit, while he hadn't even noticed any of my peculiar and no doubt annoying ways.

I wish I could say that this experience completely cured me of fault finding. It didn't. But it did make me aware early in my marriage that husbands and wives need to keep in perspective, and usually ignore, the small differences in their habits and personalities. Whenever I hear of married couples being incompatible, I always wonder if they are suffering from what I now call the Grapefruit Syndrome. (Lola B. Walters, *Ensign*, April 1993, p. 13)

President Spencer W. Kimball said: "If each spouse submits to frequent self-analysis and measures his own imperfections by the yardstick of perfection and the Golden Rule, and if each spouse sets about to correct self in every deviation found by such analysis rather than to set about to correct the deviations in the other party, then transformation comes and happiness is the result" (*Marriage and Divorce,* p. 19).

The Prophet Joseph Smith said, "I do not dwell upon your faults, and you shall not upon mine. Charity, which is love, covereth a multitude of sins" (*Teachings of the Prophet Joseph Smith,* ed. Joseph Fielding Smith [Salt Lake City: Deseret Book, 1976], p. 316).

These thoughts about examining ourselves first and avoiding criticism are consistent with the powerful message of the Savior:

"And why beholdest thou the mote that is in thy brother's eye, but considerest not the beam that is in thine own eye?

"Or how wilt thou say to thy brother, Let me pull out the mote out of thine eye; and, behold, a beam is in thine own eye?

"Thou hypocrite, first cast out the beam out of thine own eye; and then shalt thou see clearly to cast out the mote out of thy brother's eye" (Matthew 7:3–5).

Casting blame on our spouse for the problems in our marriage is an easy trap to fall into. We need to remind ourselves constantly of our need to look inward and to avoid the "Grapefruit Syndrome."

Another woman shared this meaningful counsel she received:

> Although my husband was an excellent father, I often felt irritated and angry. I wanted him to fit the image of what I thought he should be. I had certain ideals and goals I wanted implanted in him.
>
> One day, I turned to my father for advice. Because of his training as a psychiatrist, I knew he wouldn't be

too critical of his son-in-law. His first words were like a cold-water dunking: "Martha, if you continue like this, you could drive your husband away."

My jaw dropped. "What do you mean by that?" *This wasn't going at all as I'd expected.*

He held up his hand to ward off my indignation. "Just let me explain on a matter that is different, but the principle is the same. Not long ago, I was counseling a Latter-day Saint woman who had left a basically good marriage. She felt her husband wasn't living all the Church standards. Years of nagging and pleading hadn't changed him. She thought that leaving him would force him to change his ways in order to win her back. She never suspected that he would find someone else who loved and respected him as he was. He remarried happily after their divorce, and she was devastated."

Why am I getting this lecture? I thought. I had never considered leaving my husband. *Why was I suddenly in the wrong?* My chin went up. "Are you saying I should just quit pushing, and forget my own ideals?" I asked defensively.

"No, I'm saying lead but don't drive. Be gentle in your persuasion while recognizing his strengths and achievements. Be an example without criticizing. In your rush to achieve your goals, you may be sending a silent message that he's not measuring up. He's a good man, Martha, and he needs to know that you think so, too. . . .

"Patience and love are eternal, too." He opened his scriptures and read: "No power or influence can or ought to be maintained by virtue of the priesthood, only by persuasion, by long-suffering, by gentleness and meekness, and by love unfeigned;

"By kindness, and pure knowledge, which shall greatly enlarge the soul without hypocrisy, and without guile." (D&C 121:41–42.) . . .

"These two verses," he explained, "contain the ele-

ments for success in *any* relationship—and especially
the relationship between husband and wife." (Martha
Macfarlane Wiser, *Ensign,* April 1989, pp. 17–18)

Years ago, the youth organization in the Church was
called "The Mutual Improvement Association," or the
MIA. Ideally, that is what a good marriage ought to be—a
mutual improvement association. We should do all we
can to help each other improve in the most effective way.
We really can help shape each other if we do as we
should. If we work to accentuate the positive, we can
progress together.

One wife shared how this process had worked in her
own marriage: "Before I was married, I didn't have a very
good opinion of myself. My self-esteem was not what I
would have liked it to be. I was always putting myself
down. Much of what I have developed in that area of my
life has come since I married Ed. He has always supported
me and has made me feel that I was special. I'm sure that
there are things he doesn't particularly like about me but
he never speaks negatively or makes me feel that I was
anything but what I ought to be. As a result, I find myself
trying to be better in every way and my love for him
keeps growing." When both partners in a marriage feel
that way, mutual improvement can occur.

There are many in the divorce courts who are saying or
thinking, "If my partner would change, we could probably make a go of this marriage." Generally, there is
enough fault to go around. As someone once said, "It is a
mighty thin pancake that doesn't have two sides." We
need to enter into a healthy dose of self-analysis, as the
disciples did in the upper room when Jesus said that one
among them would betray him, and each one asked,
"Lord, is it I?" (Matthew 26:22).

We can and must come to realize the eternal importance of our marriages and develop the capacity to over-

look each other's faults. As we invite the Spirit of the Lord to be with us, we can come to realize more fully that our companions are literal children of our Heavenly Father. The most important association in all the world to help us become like him is our sacred marriage relationship. When we truly understand this, we will commit ourselves to join the construction team and not be on the wrecking crew. We will avoid "ceaseless pinpricking."

Keep Your Courtship Alive

Your relationship with your companion is, throughout your life and even in the end, the treasure that will be of most enduring value. "Our marriage relationships ought to be a top priority. Our marriages ought to come before everything but our relationships with God" (*Church News,* July 7, 1990, p. 16).

As a couple, you need to find time to do things together—just the two of you. As important as it is to be with the children as a family, you also need regular weekly time alone together. Scheduling that time will let your children know that your love for each other is important. It takes some doing: planning, scheduling, and investing resources. Such dates don't need to be costly, however. The time together is the most important element.

Jane McBride Choate, a dedicated mother of four children, wrote of the importance of a couple's planning occasions for just the two of them to be together:

> Swimming lessons, gymnastics, reading, Young Women, basketball, Scouting, piano lessons, Church activities—believe it or not, we did them all! Larry and I firmly believed that our four children should learn new skills and that we should be involved in their

activities. We were careful to hold daily family prayer and enjoyed many other family activities. Larry had a regular "date" night when he would take one of the children on an outing. Larry baby-sat when I was involved in my Church calling. All in all, we had an active, demanding family life.

Somewhere along the way, when I was chauffeuring our daughter to one activity while Larry was taking a son to another, we realized that all was not quite right. We were doing *too much*. We were committed to our children—we wanted to be great parents—but we were missing something just as important. Where was the extra time or a spare weekend for Larry and me—just the two of us?

As we examined our lives, we realized that what we thought was a strength was actually a weakness: there was much time for our children, but very little for ourselves. Our prayers, for instance, always focused on the children, and our activities always included the children. We realized that we had not had time away together since our first child was born. Though we were trying to be devoted parents, we knew that our efforts would backfire if our marriage was weak.

So we quickly arranged to trade baby-sitting with another family and took a short getaway. Though we traveled only sixty miles and had just one night and one day together, the benefits were tremendous. Larry and I talked about everything—our goals, our work, our successes and milestones, our problems. We learned that the incessant demands of daily life had preempted much of what we used to talk about. On our return, we discovered that the children, too, had benefited from their short vacation from us.

After that, we worked to more reasonably balance time for the children and time for Larry and me. How painful it was to review our involvement with the children's activities and decide what to drop! With more open time, one of the first things we did was to start dating each other again. As we've worked *ourselves* back into our lives, we've discovered that the children have not suffered. In fact, I think they're happier now because Larry and I are happier—and more rested. (*Ensign*, August 1989, p. 47)

One morning at the Missionary Training Center, I greeted one of the senior missionaries who had entered just a few days before. I said, "Good morning, brother. How is it going?" I wasn't prepared for his candid response.

"This is the hardest thing I have ever done in my life!"

"Why is that?"

"Being together with my wife twenty-four hours a day for the first time is really a tough assignment. You see, we entered the MTC just a few days after I retired from work. I was good at making the money and she was good at spending it. I had a good business and spent a lot of time working at it and she pretty well took care of raising our children. She went her way and I went mine. But now— twenty-four hours a day! This has got to be the biggest challenge I have faced since we got married. I hope we make it."

Frankly, I don't know how they adjusted to each other during the next year or so. But of this I am sure: they hadn't, up to that point, built a relationship between the two of them that would make them comfortable together even for a full day, let alone an eternity.

In contrast to that experience, I remember the day a friend of mine came into my office. He and his wife had been married for more than thirty years. The conversation went something like this:

"Joe, I've just come from the doctor's office where we were told that Edith will have to undergo some serious surgery in the next few days. The doctors say there's a 50 percent chance that she will not make it." He obviously was very worried. "You know, Joe," he went on, "this whole thing has caused me a lot of thought. Before long, all the children will be married, and even though we believe that families are sealed together forever, the truth is that they will have families of their own. In a few years, I will be retiring and won't have to get up and go to work every morning. I've come to realize that the thing Edith and I have that is of the most value to me and, hopefully, to us, is our relationship. I've never felt this so strongly."

He dropped his head down toward his knees and, with his hands clutched tightly together almost as if he were uttering a prayer, said, "If Edith can only make it, I'm going to do everything I can to let her know how important she is to me. I'm going to do all I can to make our relationship closer than it has ever been."

I visited with them not long ago, and there is no doubt that they are doing very well. They have been blessed to form a close, enduring relationship.

The day may well come, as your children leave home, that you and your companion will be left with just the two of you to enjoy your positive relationship—or to suffer if you haven't really worked to develop one. Hopefully, you will come to feel deeply that you have married your best friend and that there is no one on earth or in heaven with whom you would rather be.

In the process of marriage, we need to make conscious efforts to continue the courtship and always remember the importance of expressing our affection. Once when my father-in-law was leaving the house after lunch to return to the field to work, my mother-in-law said, "Albert, you get right back in here and tell me you love me." He grinned and jokingly said, "Elsie, when we were married, I told you I loved you, and if that ever changes, I'll let you know."

It's hard to overuse the expression, "I love you." Remember, the Lord said: "A new commandment I give unto you, That ye love one another; as I have loved you, that ye also love one another. By this shall all men know that ye are my disciples, if ye have love one to another" (John 13:33–34). As Christ's disciples, his commandment to love one another applies to us in a general sense as well as specifically in our marriages.

The word *love* is difficult to understand in English, Spanish, Portuguese, and probably a number of other languages with which I am not familiar. For example, I could say to an acquaintance or to an entire congregation, "I love you," and mean it sincerely. When I use those exact same words speaking to my wife, Barbara, the message is very different. We need to know who is speaking to whom and in what context to know what we mean by the word *love.*

The Greeks don't have this problem because they have three words that express different kinds of love. Knowing these words and what they mean can be important to our marriage.

The first Greek word is *eros,* or romantic love. This is the kind of love that attracts a person to a member of the opposite sex. It is the kind of love we should cultivate to keep our courtship alive. This important dimension of love is truly significant in strengthening a marriage. The English word *erotic* comes from that Greek root.

The second kind of love is *philia.* In expressing love to a friend, an acquaintance, or a whole congregation, you would likely use this word or one of its derivatives. This kind of love is essentially horizontal in nature. It includes friends, brothers, sisters, associates, and neighbors. The Lord referred to this type of love when he commanded us to love our neighbors. It is brotherly love—in fact, Philadelphia, the "city of brotherly love," gets its name from this Greek root.

Finally, the third type of love is *agape.* Some define this dimension of love as "godlike." It is exemplified by our

Father in Heaven's capacity to love us even though we don't do everything we should all the time. This is the word used in the Greek text of the New Testament each time the Lord commands us to love our enemies. It is the type of love that allows us to overlook our companion's faults or shortcomings while we work to strengthen our relationship.

If we are serious about keeping our courtship alive and developing the type of relationship that will bring joy and happiness forever, we need to stress the importance of developing love in all three dimensions—romantic love, true friendship or companionship, and charitable, Christlike love. Any marriage in difficulty has broken down in one or more of these three areas.

If people do not cultivate love in all three dimensions in marriage, their spouses might find someone in the workplace or elsewhere who, as is often said, "understands" them. Over time their eyes and hearts may wander, and they may grow apart.

As we do all we can to keep romantic love alive, we need to avoid letting romantic affection for or attraction toward anyone else come between us as spouses. Years ago, President Harold B. Lee shared a personal experience with me that has had a powerful influence on how I conduct my relationships with members of the opposite sex in church and the workplace. The episode illustrates the importance of avoiding even the appearance of impropriety. As nearly as I recall, President Lee's sharing of the account went like this:

"Shortly after becoming a member of the Quorum of the Twelve, I was driving to work in a heavy rainstorm. I recognized one of the secretaries who worked in the building; she was standing on the corner, apparently waiting for a bus. I thought that I might be of assistance, so I stopped and gave her a ride to the Church Office Building. I hadn't been in my office five minutes when the telephone rang. President J. Reuben Clark said, 'Kid, who was that woman who was in the car with you this morning?' I explained the situation. President Clark simply said, 'Don't ever let that happen again.' And it never did."

From then on, if he ever was to give a ride to someone of the opposite sex, he always made sure that there was at least one other person in the car with him.

Along these lines, it is prudent never to permit flirtations to occur in the workplace. Church leaders are wise to have a clerk or someone else in the outer office whenever they are counseling with a sister. There is a great peace of mind in knowing that your spouse is maintaining a stance that avoids even the appearance of inappropriate behavior. It is also wise not to provide any excuse for others to gossip.

We need to cultivate a true companionship in marriage by spending sufficient time together. The Latin root *com* means "with" and *panis* means "bread." In other words, a "companion" is one with whom we eat bread—one with whom we develop a solid relationship. To do so takes time and joint effort. We should regularly evaluate ourselves in each of the three dimensions of love and work diligently to overcome our weaknesses.

IDEA 6

Be Quick to Say, "I'm Sorry"

I disagree with the popular statement of years gone by from the book and film *Love Story:* "Love means never having to say you're sorry." To develop a solid marriage, we must be able to admit we are sorry for the mistakes we make. For some people it is very hard to form the words, "I'm sorry." Their mouths and tongues just don't seem to work that way. When conflicts in marriage arise, we should be swift to apologize and ask for forgiveness, even though we may not be totally at fault. True love is developed by those who are willing to readily admit personal mistakes and offenses.

A while ago, Barbara and I were in Provo to visit with her sister and attend a Brigham Young University basketball game. My sister-in-law and her husband live near the campus of BYU. Because of the crowds and traffic we anticipated encountering after the game, I had decided to park our car in the lot near the north exit of the Marriott Center about an hour before the game was to start. I asked Barbara if she would follow me in her sister's car and bring me back.

She said, "Why don't you just walk? It's just a few blocks."

"No, I think it is nearer to a mile, at least," I answered.

"No, it *couldn't* be a mile," she insisted. Finally, she agreed to follow me in the other car from her sister's place to the Marriott Center. When she arrived to pick me up, she noticed that the odometer showed that the distance was indeed nearly a mile.

Later, as we were driving back to Salt Lake City following the game, she said, "I have an apology to make to you. It is nearer a mile from my sister's house to the Marriott Center, more than just a few blocks. I was thinking of the football stadium and not the Marriott Center. You were right and I was wrong. I apologize."

I've thought about that experience several times since. The fact is that it was a very simple incident. It certainly would not have hurt me (in fact, it would have been good exercise) to walk that short distance. But Barbara had the ability to apologize and say that she was sorry. It's not hard to like someone who has that capacity!

When differences do arise, being able to discuss and resolve them is important, but there are instances when it is best to take a time-out. Biting our tongue and counting to ten or even to a hundred is sometimes helpful. Occasionally, even letting the sun go down on our wrath can help bring us back to the problem in the morning more rested, more calm, and with a better chance for resolution.

From time to time I hear a person say something like, "Why, we have been married for fifty years, and we have never had a difference of opinion." If that is literally the case, then either one of the partners is overly dominated by the other, or someone is a stranger to the truth. I am not suggesting that every marriage suffers from knock-down, drag-out arguments filled with contention and vindictiveness. I am referring to honest differences in how we look at things. Coming from different backgrounds and circumstances, any intelligent couple will have some differences of opinion. Our challenge is to be sure that we know how to resolve them. That is part of the process of making a good marriage better.

By suggesting that differences of opinion exist in a marriage, I do not want to be seen as guilty of tarnishing an ideal. I have known of couples who have been able to live together many years—even throughout their entire marriages—without becoming involved in serious confrontations of opinion. In those cases, rather than tarnish the ideal, they have worked to polish it, to rise above differences in wholesome ways. When offenses arise, such people are quick to say, "I'm sorry," because their relationship is so valuable to them that they do not want it to be marred by continuing negative feelings.

One effective method of dealing with differences when they do arise is to avoid judgmental statements such as: "You really have an ugly temper," or, "How could you be so insensitive?" or, "I don't like the way you do or say . . ." (whatever). When we feel offended by something our spouse has said or done, our communication will be more effective if we couch our comments in the first person, letting our spouse know how we feel personally rather than making judgmental statements.

For example, rather than saying something like, "How could you say such a thing?" try a statement like, "Sweetheart, when you say that it makes me feel . . ." (and then express your feelings). Expressing how you personally are made to feel—how you are affected—gets to the problem without attacking your mate. As a result, your spouse's self-esteem will less likely be damaged and you will have helped to resolve differences constructively.

Negative, ugly statements or judgments about each other, once voiced, cannot be called back. If we can learn to approach problems calmly, without attacking, the process of patching up the differences can be well on its way. Thus we will avoid breaking down the bridges of wholesome communication.

Learn to Live within Your Means

Some of the most difficult challenges in marriage arise in the area of finances. "The American Bar Association . . . indicated that 89 percent of all divorces could be traced to quarrels and accusations over money" (*Ensign,* July 1975, p. 72).

We live in a time when the economics that surround marriage and family are likely as challenging as they have ever been. Our society is relatively affluent. For many, two incomes have come to seem necessary to maintain the desired standard of living.

Things that in the past were seen as luxuries have become today's "necessities." For example, Barbara and I, along with our six children, had returned from presiding over a mission before we ever owned a car that had air conditioning. I don't think that any of our children would seriously consider buying a car today that did not have air conditioning.

Years ago, in a personal conversation, President Harold B. Lee said, "I feel sorry for people who are born rich or beautiful, for those are two obstacles that seldom can be overcome." A couple is blessed when, regardless of the financial circumstances in which they grew up, both husband and wife agree on the importance of managing whatever money they have available. The ability to manage money is even more important than the ability to earn it.

Marriage partners often come from differing levels of economic affluence, and so expectations may vary widely. Such differences can cause real tension in a marriage. I admired Angela, who came from an affluent family but did not fall into this problem. She grew up in a lovely home, and most things that money could buy were made available to her. While in her last year at the university, she met and fell in love with Robert, a recently returned missionary. His background economically was very different from hers. His parents had struggled to support their rather large family, and financial reverses had made it difficult to finance even some of the basics. Even with these differences, Robert and Angela decided to marry, knowing that the path ahead was not going to be easy. They talked about how they could make ends meet with part-time work, some scholarship money, and careful budgeting. They did want to do as much as possible on their own.

Unlike some in similar circumstances, Angela adjusted beautifully. She made sure that Robert always knew of her love and confidence. She was willing to change her lifestyle and did a creditable job of distinguishing between luxuries and necessities. Now Angela and Robert look back on their experiences together in those early years of marriage as some of the most rewarding of their lives. Robert's employment makes possible a comfortable living for their family, but because of the years of struggling, he and Angela are in a better position to teach their children the realities of making do on what their future spouses may be able to acquire.

If we are to achieve happiness and success in marriage, we need to learn to live within our means—whatever they may be. That may not always be easy, especially as marriages are starting out. Couples who learn to postpone or forego some purchases in order to stay within their budget make a monumental step toward happiness. I remember some counsel I received from one of my professors at the university many years ago. He said, "Joe, the best way to save money is to postpone expenses."

When we moved to Pullman, Washington, to attend graduate school, we had three children and Barbara was expecting our fourth. Major appliances did not come with the "temporary" World War II surplus housing apartments available for married students. (I say "temporary" because they were still going strong more than ten years after the war had ended.) In a used-appliance store, we found a stove and refrigerator that cost a fraction of what we would have paid for them new. Even though we had to work with a little innovation to make the latch of the refrigerator door function, the appliances served our needs very adequately for the three years it took to finish graduate school. We then sold them to incoming married students who were delighted to pay as much as we had paid for them originally. Instead of leaving graduate school with our five children and a lot of debt, we had saved enough—through part-time work, a fellowship, and a wife who knew how to make ends meet—to place a down payment on a big, old, modest home near the University of Idaho.

Barbara is a great shopper. I hardly remember her ever paying full retail price for anything. In our graduate school days, she would watch for sales, use powdered milk, and buy cheese, fruit, and vegetables in bulk, dividing the cost with other married couples who shared our poverty in student housing. She knew how to patch the boys' jeans and sew dresses for the girls that outlasted store-bought ones and were passed down to the younger children as they came along.

Even though we knew that our parents would have been willing and were in a financial condition to help us, we wanted to subsist on our own insofar as possible. Some of our choicest memories as a couple came from those years of independently struggling together to make ends meet. If some generous philanthropist had paid all our expenses for graduate school in much more posh circumstances, we would have missed that tremendous experience of growing together as a couple and family during those choice and challenging years.

One young man, shortly after he had married at an early age, discovered that his wife insisted on living in a house with a price far beyond their ability to pay at the time. She also was rarely seen in the same dress twice—even if she had to buy her clothing on credit. She had grown up in a home where apparently the philosophy had been that the way to "get ahead" was to go into debt. Needless to say, this marriage has been rocky, and at times the relationship has been stretched to the limit. Debt has plagued their lives and now, at retirement age, they are still making house payments and do not have the means to enjoy their golden years without a lot of extra stress and anxiety.

Couples who commit themselves to pay their tithing first and then to avoid debt, insofar as possible, build their marriage on a firmer financial foundation. Those who remember that spending fifty dollars a month more than they receive equals misery, and spending fifty dollars less than they receive equals happiness, avoid much stress in a marriage.

Elder Marvin J. Ashton gave some excellent counsel in a speech, later printed in a pamphlet called "One for the Money." In it, he told of interviewing a young couple engaged to be married. They seemed to be well prepared to start an eternal marriage. Each had several advantages, including college education, good homes, and cultural experiences. He was pleased with all their responses during the interview except one. When he asked, "Who is going to manage the money in your marriage?" she replied, "He is, I guess." The prospective husband responded, "We haven't talked about that yet." Elder Ashton said that the response surprised and shocked him.

Many couples enter marriage without adequately considering the importance of good joint financial planning. They would do well to get a copy of Elder Ashton's suggestions regarding financial planning and budgeting. Consider some of the major points he made:

1. Pay an honest tithing.

2. Learn to manage money before it manages you.

3. Learn self-discipline and restraint in money matters.

4. Use a budget.

5. Make education a continuing process.

6. Work toward home ownership.

7. Appropriately involve yourself in an insurance program.

8. Understand the influence of external forces, such as inflation, on family finances and investments.

9. Appropriately involve yourself in a food storage and emergency preparedness program (see *One for the Money* [Salt Lake City: Deseret Book, 1990].

In some marriages, the husband unilaterally takes care of the finances. That approach can create problems for the wife in a variety of ways. I remember visiting the home of a relatively young widow to offer our condolences at the time of the unexpected death of her husband. She said, "He always took such good care of everything. He made all those decisions. He wrote out the checks, paid the bills, did most of the shopping." Then, with a touch of desperation in her voice, she said, "Frankly, I don't have the slightest idea of what we have in the bank or where we are financially."

Our good friend had not done his wife a favor by failing to involve her in these matters. Not only was it inadvisable from a management standpoint, it was unwise in terms of her feeling like a full partner in the marriage relationship. The husband and wife should both be fully included in making financial decisions and policies. In one marriage I know of, the wife's name wasn't even on the checking account. She felt completely dependent on her husband to provide her with the money she needed even in the most minor purchases. When control of the family finances is fully taken over by one of the spouses, it places too much power and influence with one person and can cause serious problems in a relationship.

Elder Ashton wrote: "A disgusted husband once said, 'I know that in life money talks, but when my wife gets hold of it, all it ever says is good-bye.' To the husband who says his wife is the poorest money manager in the world, I would say, 'Look in the mirror and meet the world's poorest teacher-trainer'" (*One for the Money,* p. 6).

For years, the leaders of the Church have counseled that with the exception of buying a home, paying for education, or making other vital investments, we should avoid debt as we would avoid a plague. Interest charges on debt can destroy us. Someone once said that we either control interest or it will control us—we are either the victims or the victors of interest. Interest owed is a brutal taskmaster that never sleeps. Commercial advertisements make buying on credit or borrowing against the equity in your home seem easy ways to overcome financial problems or to acquire things. We should never forget that the resulting finance charges can not only destroy our financial position but also may seriously threaten our marriage.

The time may come—and better sooner than later—to get out our scissors and our credit cards, and perform what Elder Jeffrey R. Holland called some "plastic surgery" (*Ensign,* June 1986, p. 30).

Brigham Young said: "It is an old saying that a woman can throw out of the window with a spoon as fast as a man can throw into the door with a shovel; but a good housekeeper will be saving and economical, and teach her children to be good housekeepers, and how to take care of everything that is put in their charge" (*Journal of Discourses*, 12:195).

If you are interested in hundreds of workable ideas for saving money, read a delightful book entitled *The Tightwad Gazette, Promoting Thrift as a Viable Alternative Lifestyle*, by Amy Dacyczyn (New York: Villard Books, 1993).

A single mother with several children was having real financial difficulties and asked for some help in budgeting. It was discovered that she was spending more than one thousand dollars a year on prepared breakfast cereal. The analyst pointed out that she could provide even more nutritional value to her children for only fifty-eight dollars a year by buying whole wheat, cracking it in her blender, and preparing delicious warm cereal for her family. This is just one example of relatively small decisions that can help strengthen a family's economic situation.

Another area in which significant family resources can be saved is that of recreational activities. Some of them are costly, but they don't need to be. Our children still talk of their favorite family vacation, a trip that, coincidentally, was one of our most economical. We traveled across the United States with all eight of us in the family station wagon—one of those three-seated varieties that had the third seat in the back facing the rear (the least favorite spot to be, so we had a seat rotation about every hundred miles). We rented two fiberglass, clamlike containers which we clamped to the top of the car; they held the tents, sleeping bags, and baggage—one relatively small bag per person. We never had a problem finding our car in a parking lot! We camped at public and commercial campgrounds along the way. (KOA campgrounds loved us!) Over the course of twenty-two days, we stayed in motels only two nights and had sit-down meals in restaurants just two or three times.

While the boys and I put up the tents each night, the girls would prepare a hot dinner on the camp stove. For breakfast we had plenty of fresh fruit and granola. We bought the makings for sandwiches to eat along the way and pulled into rest stops in the afternoons for "watermelon busts." In upper New York, we remember the produce stands outside the fields, where we would drop a quarter in the "honor box" for a fresh head of cabbage and then cut it up and eat it raw for a refreshing and healthful treat as we traveled.

We drove across the United States to the East Coast, stopping at historic spots along the way. We will never forget Thomas Jefferson's Monticello, the Lincoln Memorial, the climb down the inside of the Washington Monument, the Capitol building, the Library of Congress, Civil War sites, and on and on. Beginning at Sharon, Vermont, the birthplace of the Prophet Joseph Smith, we traveled west through other Church history sites, including Palmyra, Kirtland, Nauvoo, Carthage, and Independence. A family testimony meeting in the quiet of the Sacred Grove in Palmyra was a spiritual experience to be remembered forever.

In retrospect, we have mostly forgotten the nights it rained, as well as the inconvenience of packing and unpacking. Even the memories of the crowded conditions in the car have long since faded. What we remember now are the togetherness, the sights, the impact of what we experienced. We remember the black mother with her four-year-old child who asked, pointing to the majestic statue of Lincoln in the Memorial, "Mommy, who is that?" The mother replied with emotion, "Why, don't you know who that is? He is the most important man in our lives!"

For a relatively modest financial investment, our family

grew in our appreciation of what it means to live in a country where freedom has been bought through the sacrifice of the blood of thousands. We learned to acknowledge the spiritual heritage of faith offered by members of the Church who had gone before. The funding for all of this was minimal.

Gain the satisfaction that comes from saving money and avoiding unnecessary expenses. Do what you can with what you have. Plugging the small leaks in the financial ship of the home can reap great benefits. If you want your marriage to be successful, remember the importance of avoiding debt insofar as possible and otherwise living within your means.

Be a True Partner in Home and Family Responsibilities

Barbara is a canner. I think she must have developed this habit from her own upbringing on the farm in Midway, Utah, where she participated in canning literally thousands of quarts of fruit and vegetables to help take care of their large family's needs during the winter. During the canning season, when I come home from the office, it is not unusual to find several bushels of pears, peaches, string beans, or tomatoes ready to be processed. Over the years, whenever we could, we have worked together on the project. I peel or slice while she takes care of the more technical work—preparing the bottles, steaming the fruit or vegetables, and caring for the pressure cooker and its intricacies. We have some of our best visits during these projects and often find ourselves reaffirming, "We are a good team."

Contrast this with the attitude of a man I'll call Roger, who felt that there was a definite division between what he called "women's" and "men's" work. The father of several children, he seemed to take pride in the fact that he had never once changed a child's diaper in all the years of his marriage. During the nights, he slept peacefully while his wife got up to feed and care for the babies. After all, he reasoned, he had to get sufficient rest to go to work the next morning and earn the living for the family. He also was the "chief financial officer." His wife received an allowance for household expenses and was strictly monitored in how well she stayed within her budget. Her name did not even appear on the checking account or credit cards.

When Roger came home, he generally assumed that his work was done and depended on his wife to wait on him. It doesn't take a psychological genius to recognize that their relationship suffered some severe stress.

On the other hand, there was Ann, who had been raised by a doting mother who made Ann's bed in the morning, straightened her bedroom, tidied up the house, and cooked the meals. Ann was attractive and intelligent. She was hired to work at a bank when she was just out of high school. She dated regularly. She married an outstanding returned missionary when she was about twenty years old, and they were blessed with several children. She would spend hours reading novels, watching soap operas, or shopping. Meals were often late or neglected altogether, and the house was generally in disarray—a source of embarrassment when company would come. She often attempted to excuse herself by saying that housekeeping and cooking were simply not her talents or interests. Anyone could conclude that their marriage relationship— although it started positively—would not be ideal.

The sharing of responsibility for home and family is vital to building a solid marriage. The husband who comes home from work and pitches in to help with projects around the house gives his wife a much-needed boost and does much to strengthen their relationship. All that we as husbands need do is to take the entire responsibility of home and children for just one full day in order to learn that not all the work is accomplished by us.

Years ago, when our children were very young, I

remember going to a store to buy a birthday gift for Barbara. As the clerk was gift-wrapping the present, she asked, "Does your wife work?" I replied, "Yes, she surely does, although it is all at home with the house and children!" Every time Barbara went to the hospital for a few days when the next addition to the family was born, leaving me to struggle with taking care of things at home, I managed at least to gain a glimpse of all that she regularly accomplished. I assure you that she was much more appreciated when she returned home from those hospital "vacations."

Each one of us needs to recognize that we are in our marriage partnership together. There is much to be done to make things work smoothly. Sharing responsibilities around the home and with the children draws us together and helps lift the burdens. Barbara and I have discovered that we can make our bed every morning in less than a minute and it's done for the day. She says that she lets me do it to help me feel good about myself all day, and I guess there may be something to that.

My mother-in-law, who gave birth to twelve children and reared a thirteenth as well, was a remarkably well-organized manager in their home. She is responsible for teaching her nine daughters all those useful homemaking skills. In her homespun way, she insisted that at least two tasks be done on time—making the beds and washing the dishes. Have you ever noticed that if the bed is made, even though there may be other items out of place, the room takes on an appearance of orderliness? If everything else is in place and the bed is not made, the room appears disheveled. It is about the same way with the dishes in the kitchen. When they are done, the whole room looks better. And regardless of the appearance of the remainder of the kitchen, if the dishes are not done, the room appears messy. Having both tasks done provides a great start for the day.

Some husbands are not in the habit of picking up their own things, hanging up their clothes, or seeing that their soiled clothing is in the hamper. One wife actually hammered some clothes hooks in the floor to make the point that that was where her husband apparently chose to "hang" his clothes. Annoyance and even resentment can develop in the one left to do these obviously personal neglected chores. "If not by me, by whom?" is a good question to ask ourselves when we see something out of place that needs attention. Each partner should take an appropriate share of the work and not bother to "keep score" about who is doing the most. If each goes more than halfway in helping with the tasks at hand, a bonding will develop that strengthens a marriage and at the same time helps to train the children.

One young mother of four children said, "I really came to look forward to Saturday mornings, when my husband would take all the children for a few hours to the park to play or out in the car to run errands with him. It gave me a chance to regroup, work on a project without interruption, or get away for a while. Another advantage was that it gave the children a chance to become better acquainted with their father. It really was a winning situation for all of us."

For some people, the anticipation of an event is often as rewarding as the realization. In our own marriage, we found that it was helpful for Barbara to know several days in advance that on Saturday morning (or whenever), I planned to be home with the children so that she could be free to leave the house and do some shopping, go to the library, run errands, or do whatever she chose. She said, "Just knowing that in advance made it easier to adjust to my daily routine." Not only was it good for her, it also provided me with some of the best experiences I have enjoyed with our children.

There are other important activities that can help make

us true partners in the home. Among them is the experience of growing together intellectually and spiritually. True partners will find time to study the scriptures together and follow this sound counsel from President Spencer W. Kimball:

"When a husband and wife go together frequently to the holy temple, kneel in prayer together in their home with their family, go hand in hand to their religious meetings, keep their lives wholly chaste, mentally and physically, . . . and both are working together for the upbuilding of the kingdom of God, then happiness is at its pinnacle" (*Marriage and Divorce* [Salt Lake City: Deseret Book, 1976], p. 24).

Part One: Summary

Success in marriage does not come automatically. Building a life together takes work and commitment and love. If we can keep in mind and strive to apply the ideas discussed in this section, we will find greater happiness and fulfillment in marriage:

1. Remember the central importance of marriage.
2. Make the Lord a partner in your marriage.
3. Learn to listen.
4. Avoid "ceaseless pinpricking."
5. Keep your courtship alive.
6. Be quick to say, "I'm sorry."
7. Learn to live within your means.
8. Be a true partner in home and family responsibilities.

I wish that everyone who marries could feel as I do. There are not adequate words to express how I feel about Barbara. She is literally my best friend. There is no one on earth with whom I would rather be—just to converse, share a sunset, or whatever. She has truly been a partner in all our endeavors. She often refers to the time when *we* were in the Air Force, or when *we* were in graduate school. Those challenging endeavors really came to be joint efforts. Her sharing has been a great strength to me over the years. On those occasions when I lacked self-confidence to do what I had been called to do, or to tackle those challenging tasks we chose for ourselves, she would give me assurance. She always made me feel that I was somehow better than my faltering self-confidence would dare to dream. It is marvelous to be married to someone you dearly love and who, in her inimitable way, lets you know that she loves you too. I hope that you feel like that about your companion now, or will come to have such feelings in the future as you work together to strengthen your marriage.

PART TWO

Building a Better Family

When Amy, our first child, was born, we were living in Charleston, South Carolina, where I was serving in the Air Force. It was during the time of the Korean War. I'll never forget how grateful we were that Barbara's mother got on a bus and made that long, four-day trip so that she could help us when Barbara and the baby came home from the hospital. I remember hearing one medical doctor say that at the time of the birth of a baby, an experienced mother or mother-in-law is worth three pediatricians. Barbara's mother had given birth to twelve children and reared a thirteenth, so she was experienced!

As we went to the hospital to pick up the new mother and daughter, my mother-in-law made a sobering statement: "Well, Joe, you and Barbara have now assumed a responsibility that you can *never* relinquish."

I've thought of that statement many times since that eventful day. As parents for the first time—and every subsequent time—we assume a tremendous responsibility. The child arrives into our lives and everything changes: schedules, priorities, goals, financial responsibilities, and a host of duties. There is no dress rehearsal. We are thrust onto the stage and the performance commences.

These little ones arrive in our homes one hundred percent dependent in every way. Following their birth, if the care of doctors, nurses, parents, or others were to be withdrawn, they would die. The awe-inspiring challenge left to us as parents is to assure that by the time our children are grown, around the ages of nineteen to twenty-one, they are virtually independent, well-educated, responsible, committed young adults who have incorporated into their lives lofty ideals. By then, hopefully, they could be called by the Lord through his prophet to serve in any mission in the world, fulfill any assignment from their mission president, and exhibit competence, diligence, and faith in their service. To accomplish all of that is not an easy challenge! Saying it is a lot easier than making it happen. As parents, we need all the help we can get.

One day following general conference, our three-year-old grandson, Andrew, asked his mother, "Mommy, is Jesus counting on me?" He must have heard someone say something like that in one of the conference speeches. His mother, Susan, assuming that this was one of those choice teaching moments, answered, "Oh yes, Andrew, Jesus is counting on you. He wants you to pick up your toys, do all the things Mommy and Daddy ask you to do, and *especially* to be kind to your little brother, Benjamin." Andrew thought about that for a few moments and then said, "Well, tell Jesus not to count on me, Mom!" Obviously, there are plenty of challenges that face parents!

Most people who marry or anticipate marrying look forward to the privilege of having children come into their lives. That aspiration is particularly true of dedicated members of The Church of Jesus Christ of Latter-day Saints, because we are blessed with an understanding of the premortal existence and the spirits there who are awaiting their opportunity to come to earth for their mortal experience.

In our own family we came to know more about this hope for children to come. Our five oldest children had married and all had children of their own. When our youngest, Spencer, returned from his mission and married his sweetheart, Sheila, they and we looked forward to having their children added to the growing family. And wait we did. I don't think there was anything that Barbara and I prayed about more regularly—every night and morning and sometimes in between. But hope and pray as we all did, there was no change in the situation.

Sometimes, when we had all the family together and the other parents were playing with or tending their children, I would look out of the corner of my eye at Spencer and Sheila and know that it was difficult for them. There were multiple medical diagnoses, including the possibility of endometriosis and the resulting fear that perhaps conceiving and carrying a baby to term would not be possible. There were visits to fertility specialists and a lot more praying and fasting. The years passed—two, three, and on to five—and their hopes were still not realized. By this time, members of the entire family—including the oldest grandchildren—were praying that someday Spencer and Sheila would have the blessing of children come into their lives.

While on assignment with the Area Presidency in Brazil, one day we received a call from Spencer with the exciting announcement that the medical tests were positive and Sheila was expecting. Then we *really* prayed, because we did not know if the pregnancy could be successfully carried to term!

Several months after returning from Brazil, we received another call from Spencer, saying that Sheila had been admitted to the Utah Valley Regional Medical Center in Provo for the delivery. He thought the baby would be born in two or three hours. We rushed to Provo and joined with the other expectant grandparents in the waiting area outside the delivery room. After nearly twelve— not two or three—hours of waiting, it happened. I don't remember ever having actually cheered before at 2:00 A.M. when I heard a baby's cry, but we did that morning!

A little later, Spencer appeared at the door of the delivery room with that beautiful new son carefully wrapped in blankets. The proud father looked so relieved, happy, and tired. The expression on his face communicated that after six long years of waiting, he and Sheila had come to the end of their problems. As some harried and challenged parents might have told them, they didn't know at *which* end of their problems they were! They had come to the front end of that marvelously challenging task of being a parent.

In the 1995 Proclamation on the Family, we read: "The first commandment that God gave to Adam and Eve pertained to their potential for parenthood as husband and wife. We declare that God's commandment for His children to multiply and replenish the earth remains in force. . . . Husband and wife have a solemn responsibility to love and care for each other and for their children. 'Children are an heritage of the Lord' (Psalms 127:3). Parents have a sacred duty to rear their children in love and righteousness, to provide for their physical and spiritual needs, to teach them to love and serve one another, to observe the commandments of God and to be law-abiding citizens wherever they live. Husbands and wives—mothers and fathers—will be held accountable before God for the discharge of these obligations."

Those whom we sustain as prophets, seers, and revelators recognize the importance and the challenge of marital and family responsibilities. They stand ready to be of assistance to us as parents, as indicated in a survey of general conference messages from 1950 to 1992. It was inter-

esting to note that when we searched a computer data-
base of those conference addresses for the words *marriage,*
family, parents, and *children,* we found those words mentioned 16,776 times, or, on average, approximately 200
times in each general conference! The strengthening of
families, marriages, and parent-child relationships is obviously a high priority in the minds of the Brethren.

In addition to the words and teachings of Church leaders, what a blessing it is to have the scriptures and other
helps that come to us through the gospel and the Church!
I don't know of any scripture that was more sobering to
me as a new parent than Doctrine and Covenants 68:25:
"And again, inasmuch as parents have children in Zion,
or in any of her stakes which are organized, that teach
them not to understand the doctrine of repentance, faith
in Christ the Son of the living God, and of baptism and
the gift of the Holy Ghost by the laying on of the hands,
when eight years old, the sin be upon the heads of the
parents." That places some heavy responsibilities directly
upon us as parents.

Recently I visited with a friend who said, "You know,
raising a family isn't easy, but in the end, the family is
really where it all is. I can't imagine how different my life
would have been without my family. It didn't take me
long to realize that there isn't anything my wife and I
wouldn't be willing to do if we thought it would help any
one of our children. We soon came to know that the
greatest joys can come when things in the family seem to
be going well—and, on the other hand, the greatest dis-
appointment and pain can come when there is some kind
of problem in the family."

The ideas that follow are offered in the solemn recog-
nition that these are not easy times. It is difficult to rear
a righteous family in today's world—but we must do all
we can. Our eternal happiness depends largely on the
efforts we make in our mortal families.

Do Not Underestimate the Power of Evil

Not long ago, I had an impromptu conversation with a group of young parents who exhibited a great deal of anxiety about rearing their children in our morally polluted environment. They asked for assistance in helping children find their way in a world that seems to be unraveling.

We all hear and read a great deal these days about our polluted physical environment—acid rain, smog, toxic wastes. But those parents recognized that there is another kind of pollution that is much more dangerous—the moral and spiritual.

In a conference address, Elder Boyd K. Packer said, "As we test the *moral* environment, we find the *pollution* index is spiraling upward" (*Ensign,* May 1992, p. 66). The Apostle Paul foresaw "that in the last days perilous times shall come" (2 Timothy 3:1). And speaking of the last days, the prophet Moroni declared, "Yea, it shall come in a day when there shall be great pollutions upon the face of the earth" (Mormon 8:31).

The effects of this great pollution are perhaps most evident in the mass media, films, television, and popular music. Of this, United States Senator Robert Byrd said: "If we in this nation continue to sow the images of murder, violence, drug abuse, . . . perversion, [and] pornography . . . before the eyes of millions of children, year after year and day after day, we should not be surprised if the foundations of our society rot away as if from leprosy" (Michael Medved, *Hollywood vs. America* [New York: Harper Perennial, 1992], p. 194).

Although there are some uplifting exceptions, in most areas of the mass media there seems to be a declaration of war against almost everything the majority of people treasure most: the family, religion, and patriotism. Marriage is degraded, while premarital and extramarital relations are encouraged and glamorized. Profanity and the foulest of vulgar gutter language bombard the ears of all who listen. Reportedly, in one R-rated movie, the most common, vulgar, four-letter word was spoken 256 times! Human life itself is trivialized by the constant barrage of violence and killings.

The fact is that today we are suffering the effects of a "plague" that has attacked our society on many fronts. President Gordon B. Hinckley described several situations in which our youth today find themselves—all of which give us as parents additional challenges. He said:

> Some time ago I read a letter to a newspaper editor which was highly critical of the Church. I have forgotten the exact language, but it included a question something like this: "When are the Mormons going to stop being different and become a part of the mainstream of America?"
>
> About this same time there came to my desk a copy of an address given by Senator Dan Coats of Indiana. He spoke of a study made by "a commission of educational, political, medical and business leaders" dealing with the problems of American youth. The committee issued a report called *Code Blue*. That report, according to the Senator, concluded: "Never before has one gen-

eration of American teenagers been less healthy, less cared for, or less prepared for life than their parents were at the same age." He went on to say, "I have seen the parade of pathologies—they are unending and increasing:

"Suicide is now the second leading cause of death among adolescents, increasing 300 percent since 1950.

"Teen pregnancy has risen 621 percent since 1940. More than a million teenage girls get pregnant each year. Eighty-five percent of teenage boys who impregnate teenage girls eventually abandon them.

"The teen homicide rate has increased 232 percent since 1950. Homicide is now the leading cause of death among fifteen- to nineteen-year-old minority youth. . . .

"Every year substance abuse claims younger victims with harder drugs. A third of high school seniors get drunk once a week. The average age for first-time drug use is now thirteen years old."

The report reached a shocking conclusion. It said: "The challenges to the health and well-being of America's youth are not primarily rooted in illness or economics. Unlike the past, the problem is not childhood disease or unsanitary slums. The most basic cause of suffering . . . is profoundly self-destructive *behavior.* Drinking. Drugs. Violence. Promiscuity. A crisis of behavior and belief. A crisis of character." (*Imprimis,* Sept. 1991, p. 1.)

When I read those statements, I said to myself, If that is the mainstream of American youth, then I want to do all in my power to persuade and encourage our young people to stay away from it. (*Ensign,* May 1992, pp. 69–70)

Every day, as our children leave home for school or other activities, they need to be strengthened against a multitude of negative influences. For example, in an unsuccessful effort to ward off teen pregnancy and sexually transmitted diseases, some organizations freely distribute birth control devices. I am convinced that this practice strongly communicates the basic message: "Anything goes; just protect yourself in the process."

It is no wonder that young parents become anxious as they attempt to fulfill their sacred trust in the face of such an onslaught of despicable influences. Unfortunately, these challenges confront members of the Church as well as nonmembers.

Parents who really want to receive assistance must return to the basics—the fundamentals of the gospel. We cannot sit complacently by and hope that things will all work out. We must be aware of the power of evil in the world so that we will constantly be on guard against it.

IDEA 2

Set Clear
Moral Standards
and Guidelines

One of the difficult tasks parents face is setting standards of morality for the family. We need to learn not to be afraid to provide clear guidelines for appropriate behavior.

An appropriate first step is to be able to say no when it is needed. As Dr. John Rosemond counseled: "Give your children regular, daily doses of Vitamin N. This vital nutrient consists simply of the most character-building two-letter word in the English language—'No.' . . . Unfortunately, many, if not most, of today's children suffer from Vitamin N deficiency. They have been over-indulged by well-meaning parents who have given them far too much of what they want and far too little of what they truly need" (*John Rosemond's Six-Point Plan for Raising Happy, Healthy Children* [Kansas City, Mo.: Andrews & McMeel, 1989], p. 114).

Even though our children say: "Well, everyone else is going to stay out until one or two in the morning, and their parents don't care. Why can't I? Don't you trust me?" we need to let them know that there are some things that members of our family simply do not do. Some parents seem to be almost pathologically concerned about their children's popularity and social acceptance, and they permit many things that are really against their better judgment: expensive fads, immodest clothes, late hours, dating before age sixteen, R-rated movies, and so on. For children and parents, standing up for what is right may be lonely at times. There may be evenings alone, parties missed, and movies unseen. It may not always be pleasant. But parenting is not a popularity contest. Your children may be frustrated at first, but ultimately they will grow to appreciate you even more because you cared enough about them to set some wholesome guidelines and standards.

You may need to get together with the parents of your children's friends and mutually agree on acceptable standards of entertainment, hours, and activities. When discussions about standards are held, either at home or with the neighbors, involve the children as well whenever possible. If they have a part in the decisions made, they will more likely "own" them and be more inclined to live up to them.

Once, on a stake conference assignment in California, I was visiting with the stake president during lunch. He told of a discussion he and his wife had held with their beautiful teenage daughter about the standards she should maintain while on her dates. "Half-jokingly, I told my daughter that if she went clear through high school without kissing a boy, I would give her 500 dollars," he said. "Well, she agreed and took me *very* seriously. When she was near graduating, after one of the big dances of the year, when her date was delivering her home, he apparently let her know that he would like to kiss her. She said, 'I can't kiss you. You're not worth it!' Apparently that agreement is going to cost me, because she is still holding me to it."

When our oldest granddaughter turned sixteen and was invited by a popular young man to go to the Senior Prom, it was quite an experience for everyone. A lot of thought and planning went into the long, beautiful formal that she and her mother were able to sew. It was crucial to get just the right necklace, earrings, hairstyle, and all the other things girls worry about.

At the appointed time the young man, a graduating senior, arrived at the door with corsage in hand to add to the special nature of the event. Traditionally, on that one night of the year many of the seniors made it a point to stay out very late—all night, in some cases. That was one of the concerns the parents had, but they had not discussed specifically if this should be a night when staying out past the usual curfew would be acceptable.

As the young man escorted our granddaughter to the car, he asked, "Uhhh, what time is your curfew? When do you have to get in?"

Not having considered this item with the family—especially on such an occasion as the Senior Prom—she stammered, "Well, uhhh . . . at least by one o'clock."

"Oh," he responded. "Well, I have to be in by twelve!" And they were.

What a blessing it is when parents can work at setting high standards with their children! When the norms among friends seem to be low, it is a strength to have parents and children agree on some higher standards. That process helps get around the excuse often given by the youth, "Well, that is what the other kids' parents let them do, so why can't I?"

Children can often be cruel to each other in social settings. Sometimes they make fun of those who have some handicap, or those who may be out of the "inner social circle." Some children are left out of parties when everyone else seems to be going. Standards need to be set among young children as well as those who are older. With training, even those young ones can be taught to observe higher social standards.

In this area, I always appreciated what Barbara taught our children about parties or any group activity sponsored by our family. She said, "Be sure to invite *everyone*. Don't leave anyone out—even the ones you may not like as well as the others." That standard helped ease a lot of social pain among young acquaintances. Children who are trained young to have empathy for others will likely carry that trait over into their adult lives as well.

Not only should the standards of moral behavior be set and taught, they should also be shown by parental example. An experience I had the year I left home for the first time to attend Utah State Agricultural College—all of forty miles away—taught me the value of my parents' example.

During that summer after high school graduation, I had just turned seventeen. At that time I probably didn't weigh more than 120 pounds soaking wet. No one was recruiting me to play football for anyone! I needed some cash, and so I went to the First Security Bank in Logan to write out one of the first checks I had ever written in my life. It was an out-of-town and even an out-of-state check, to be drawn from the First Security Bank branch in Preston, Idaho. I was a little nervous and I must have looked younger than the average person with a checking account. The lady who served at the teller window peered at me over the bifocal eyeglasses perched on her nose and said, "Hmmm . . . wait just a minute."

A few moments later she returned, and I was ushered into the bank president's office. He sat there like a judge with his elbows firmly planted on the huge desk in front of him and his chin resting on his hands. He studied me with his piercing eyes for what seemed like a long time.

Then he said, "What is your name, boy?"

"Joe Christensen. A lot of people call me 'Junior.'"

"Where are you from?"

"Banida, Idaho—it's . . . it's just north of Preston."

"Who is your father?"

"Joseph A. Christensen."

He drew a deep breath and, in a much more relaxed manner, leaned back in his chair, cupped his hands behind his head, smiled, and said something I think I will never forget:

"I know your father. He is an honest and a hard-working man. You can write out your check for any amount you need."

I realized that I had been given a priceless gift that I had not earned—I had reaped where I hadn't sown.

Since then, I have recognized the value of a parent's example. I have had in the past and still retain a desire to set that kind of example for our children. I hope that being my son or daughter would never be a handicap to our children or, now, even to our grandchildren. Perhaps as helpful as any other thing we could do to assist our children in maintaining high moral standards would be to set a good example for them. If we never do anything we would not want them to do, we will have shown the way.

Teach Your
Children to Work

Teaching children to work, to take responsibility, requires some creativity. Especially in urban settings, too many children are growing up in an environment where they do not have enough to do. They are like
the thirteen-year-old boy who was asked what he did all
day in the summer.

He said, "Well, I get up in the morning about ten or
eleven. Then my mom gets me something to eat. Then
maybe I'll go with some of the guys and play a little basketball, maybe watch TV, and then go down to the mall
and 'hang out' for a while—sorta watch the girls and
stuff."

When asked what time he got to bed, he said, "Oh,
usually about one or two o'clock. I go over to a friend's
house and watch some videos. It's really neat, because my
friend's mom told the guy at the video shop that it was
all right for her son to check out any video he wanted—
including R-rated."

We could well feel great concern for the future of that
young Latter-day Saint boy and his friends.

Years ago, I discovered from personal experience that
parents can do much to create work for their children. I
grew up on a farm in Banida, Idaho. During my early teen

years, World War II was in full swing. It was difficult for my father to find hired help, because almost all the available men from our little town were serving in the armed forces. As a result, the responsibility that rested on the shoulders of my younger brother Wade, our cousin Blaine (who was my age and grew up with us), and me was greater than it otherwise might have been. We boys, as well as my older sister, Coy, had to assume heavier duty than would have been expected of most teenagers.

I can vividly remember Dad coming to our bedroom door every morning at six o'clock sharp and saying, "Boys, boys, it's time to get up and get going." It didn't matter what the weather was or how late we had gotten in the night before. Especially on those cold days when the temperature fell below zero, the warmth and comfort of the bed was hard to leave, but sleeping in was not an option. Rain, snow, cold, or whatever, we knew that we would have to hurry to get through the milking, feeding, and cleaning up in time to catch the old, rattletrap school bus that would carry us on all the stops through Banida and Winder and the twelve miles to school in Preston.

When school ended, we couldn't lallygag around. We had to be on our way, even though there were some friends—of both genders—with whom we would have liked to spend more time. There were also activities in which we would have liked to be involved, but we knew that we had to be on that school bus so we could get home to do the chores. No one else was around to take our place. Even in the summers, when we had spent most of the daylight hours out in the fields driving tractors, hauling hay, or irrigating, we always knew that the milking and other associated chores had to be done when we got back to the house. Taking care of that herd of cows was the perennial activity that was a constant in the memory of my adolescent years.

As the war came to a close, wheat and milk prices rose

and the family income significantly improved. Dad and Mom were even able to invest in more farmland at that time.

You can imagine what I thought when, some years later, I inadvertently overheard a conversation my father was having with an uncle who had come to visit.

Dad said, "Well, we could have been getting along all right without even keeping the herd of milk cows, but Goldie and I decided that we wanted to have something the boys would need to do every morning and every night. We thought it would be good for them."

I thought then, "You mean, Dad and Mom, that through so many of those years you thought we needed a *make-work* project?"

Although I didn't fully appreciate it then, I can see now that those farm chores brought into our lives some of the best experiences and training I had while growing up. Work became a friend and a protector from idleness and bad habits.

Barbara has written about how her mother helped her and her eight sisters in the area of work: "Mother taught us the *joy of work*—not just the importance of hard work, but the joy of it. We all worked hard in our home. I have blessed her name all my life for one of the most important things she taught me. Many people work and work hard, but I have decided that there are lots of people who don't enjoy working. My parents had no use for laziness. They taught us that there is no such thing as a spiritually strong person who is at the same time lazy. Mother taught us the *magic of the early hours* of the morning for accomplishment. She often told us that 'those who are up early run ahead all day.' She always suggested that we as young mothers should arise a while before the remainder of the family. So much can be accomplished during those moments alone. She often showed us the beauty of the early morning. Sometimes we had to see it through our half-opened eyes, I admit. However, to this day I can feel a bit of excitement early in the morning when I think of that quiet time when meditating is easier, studying is more profitable, and one seems to accomplish twice as much as later on in the day."

When rearing children in an urban setting, it is more difficult to find opportunities to teach them how to work. We didn't have a yard large enough to plant much of a vegetable garden, but long before we heard President Spencer W. Kimball urge the Saints to plant gardens, we knew that such an enterprise could help us teach our family how to work. We looked around the neighborhood and found that on Sunnyside Avenue, right across from the married students' chapel, there was a vacant lot. We will always be grateful to the Wheelwrights, who permitted us to plant a garden in the vacant space while they were waiting to build their home on it. We arranged to get the water to irrigate the garden from a hose attached to one of their neighboring rental apartments, with an understanding that they would be most welcome to share the vegetables with us.

During the next few years, as a result of the early and late hours spent plowing, tilling, planting, cultivating, weeding, harvesting, and hauling manure and leaves to fertilize the soil, we found many opportunities to teach our children. Not only did they learn the joy and rewards of work, but they also discovered that vegetables don't just come from the grocery-store shelf. The children enjoyed sharing ripe, fresh vegetables with the neighbors.

During those choice gardening years, President Marion G. Romney regularly passed by our garden during his early-morning summer walks. He would frequently comment about how the garden was progressing. On one occasion, mention was made of our garden during a conversation with other General Authorities. President Romney said, "I've watched their garden grow. I've even eaten vegetables from it." With a twinkle in his eye, he added, "And some of them they have *given* me." He had a marvelous sense of humor.

For some of our children, the garden was just an exercise in learning to work. But a few of them developed an appreciation for planting and watching things grow that they have passed down in turn to their own children. When the Wheelwrights finally decided that they would build on their lot, they dug the footings and basement through some mighty fine and fertile soil that had served our family well for a number of those growing-up years.

Being with and teaching our children how to work is important. Our daughter Linda mentioned, "My friend's mother would often give orders to her daughter just as she was going out the door for a shopping trip, 'When I get back, I expect that you will have the whole house all cleaned and straight.'

"For my friend, work was always a drudge and she grew up holding feelings of resentment toward her mother. Instead, my mom always worked with us and taught us how to do it. I remember one day when she took me into the bathroom with the cloths, brushes, mop bucket, soap, and cleaning materials and showed me how to clean the floor, tub, toilet, and sink. I didn't have to experiment and learn all of that without someone working with me. She always said, 'Whenever you are cleaning, be sure to take care of the corners and the rest of the room will almost take care of itself'—and then she showed me how to do it."

In addition to the gardening, the boys would line up lawn mowing and snow shoveling jobs. I remember in the heat of one summer when Anne, a young doctor, moved in next door. Before they had completely moved in her furniture, she reported that Spencer, who was then about seven years old, had come over and said, "Boy, in the winter it sure snows a lot around here! Do you think you will need someone to shovel your walks?"

Our oldest son, Stephen, graduated from high school a few months before he turned nineteen. He bought an old, rusty Ford pickup and an edger, borrowed the family's lawn mower, and set up a business doing yard work for a long list of customers. With that and some house painting and cleaning jobs, he earned enough to take care of the expenses of his mission. We notice that those traits of industry and entrepreneurship remain with him today, long after he has completed his law degree.

The Howell family, friends of ours, have ten children. Eight of them have fulfilled missions already, and the ninth is preparing to leave before long. We were visiting with the parents about how they taught their children to work. In addition to the jobs the sons and daughters were able to get—including serving as waiters and waitresses at a local restaurant—they got involved in some extended-family collating projects for a company that produced learning materials. They said, "All of our children were involved in this and worked together. Over a period of about two years, we earned about $35,000. We used about $10,000 for a special trip for the entire extended family. The rest of the money was placed in a special mission account, to be used for nothing else. Each of the grandchildren knows that he or she will receive $1,000 from that special account when he or she goes on a mission."

These children learned more than the joy of working together. From the earliest age, they spoke of *when* they go on their missions rather than *if* they would go. They realized something of the value and rewards of work, and when they left for their missions they had acquired the capacity to work hard.

While serving as a mission president, I saw clearly how much easier the adjustment was for missionaries who had learned to work. They were more disciplined and much more successful.

When one missionary was asked why he had come home after being in the mission field for only two months, he said, "That's hard work, and I don't know how to work hard. I've never had to do anything hard in my life." Hopefully, our children and grandchildren can avoid that problem.

As mentioned, it is not always easy to teach children to work when we live in a city, but it is possible, and we should do all we can to accomplish the task. President Kimball has counseled:

"The idle generation! Hours each day and nothing to do. . . . We want you parents to create work for your children. . . .

"Do the shopping, work in the hospital, help the neighbors and the church custodian, wash dishes, vacuum the floors, make the beds, get the meals, learn to sew (and cook).

"Read good books, . . . clean the house, press your clothes, rake the leaves, shovel the snow, peddle papers."

Then he concludes: "Lawmakers in their overeagerness to protect the child have legislated until the pendulum has swung to the other extreme. But no law prohibits most work [here] suggested . . . , and parents can make work" (*The Teachings of Spencer W. Kimball,* ed. Edward L. Kimball [Salt Lake City: Bookcraft, 1982], pp. 360–61).

Some parents make the mistake of overindulging their children. One couple explained: "We didn't have much money when our older children were growing up, and so they had to work for what they received. Then things started going better for us, and we made a serious mistake with our youngest son, who was the only child at home. We gave him much more than was really good for him. He was the one who got his own car. We financed his dates. He didn't have to get a part-time job like the others, because we had a lot more then. We made it too easy for David and we now see that it wasn't good for him."

It is the exceptional well-to-do couple who can rear their children with a proper sense of material values, particularly the worth of work.

Another way to help children learn self-discipline is by involving them in such activities as learning to play a musical instrument or to master some other demanding skill. I am reminded of the story of the salesman who came to a house one hot summer day. Through the screen door, he could see a young boy practicing his scales on the piano. His baseball glove and hat were by the side of the piano bench. The salesman said, "Say, boy, is your mother home?" to which the boy replied, "What do you think?" Thank heavens for conscientious parents!

Every child should be helped to develop some skill or talent by which he or she can experience success and thus help build self-esteem. During our years at the Missionary Training Center in Provo, we noted that, without question, the missionaries who had learned to work hard and had developed self-discipline were generally much more successful in their missionary efforts. I had talked to so many of the missionaries at the MTC who were having a difficult time adjusting to getting up at 6:00 A.M. to start their daily activities. However, in one conversation with an elder who, as I recall, was from Burley, Idaho, I said, "Well, I guess it is quite an adjustment getting up so early to start the day, isn't it?" He replied, "Oh no. This is great, getting to sleep in until 6:00. At home we started milking at 4:30!" The adjustment to mission life was not nearly as hard for him as it was for many others.

Children can be taught to work. They can be given opportunities to stretch themselves and to grow through accomplishing and learning. It is not always easy—for parents or children—but the rewards of teaching these skills far outweigh the difficulties!

IDEA 4

Create an Environment in Which Spiritual Experiences Can Occur

Our prophets and leaders have suggested many simple things parents can do to help create a spiritual environment in the home. For example: Remember family prayer every day. With schedules as they are, you may need to have more than one prayer. Sending children out of your home without the spiritual protection of prayer is like sending them out into a blizzard without sufficient clothing.

Hold family home evenings *every week* without fail. This is a wonderful time to share your testimony with your children. Give them an opportunity to share their feelings about the gospel. Help them learn to recognize when they feel the presence of the Spirit. Family home evenings will help create an island of refuge and security within your own home.

Don't get discouraged if not every family home evening is a great success. Barbara and I discovered that a problem-free home evening is not always easy to achieve, especially with six children whose ages cover a wide span. Our sessions were not always filled with those "golden moments" parents hope for. I came to resonate to a tongue-in-cheek comment made by a friend who had a large family: "We often start by singing 'Love at Home' and end with 'Master, the Tempest Is Raging.'" But with regularity, planning, assignments that involve the children, and earnest prayer for the Spirit to be with you, some of the sweetest and most uplifting experiences imaginable can be had by all.

There were occasions during our family home evening lessons when one of our teenage sons appeared to be uninterested in what was going on. But later, when we would ask questions, he would surprise us by remembering details of the lesson as well as or better than almost anyone else. That experience taught me that we should not give up. We should not assume that our children are failing to absorb important ideas during our evenings together. Some value can come merely by our consistency.

One of the most important strengths our children can develop is to have their own personal spiritual experiences. We should stress the value of our children's having a direct personal involvement in such activities as reading the scriptures and praying on their own, thus developing their own testimonies. When they become personally involved in spiritual experiences, they are much more likely to avoid harmful behaviors such as cheating, lying, shoplifting, taking drugs, and breaking the law of chastity. We really have come to the day when neither we nor our children can live on "borrowed light."

Elder Harold B. Lee shared these thoughts from an early Church leader, Heber C. Kimball: "Let me say that many of you will see the time when you will have all the trouble, trial, and persecution you can stand, and plenty of opportunities to show that you were true to God and his work. This Church will have many close places through which it will have to pass before the work of God is crowned with victory. To meet the difficulties that are coming, it will be necessary for you to have a knowledge of the truth of this work for yourselves. The difficulties of this work will be of such a character that a man or woman who does not possess this personal knowledge will fall" (in Conference Report, October 1955, p. 56).

The conclusion that young people need to gain their own testimonies from their own personal experiences is affirmed in an interesting study conducted by BYU's Center for Studies of the Family, which recently reported on a sampling of 1500 Latter-day Saint youth living along the East Coast of the United States, where members of the Church are definitely in a minority. The LDS youth, compared with young people in general, experienced significantly lower rates of "delinquent behaviors," for example, offenses against others, property, morality, and the Word of Wisdom. The authors of the study concluded that the teaching of religion does have an impact on the behavior of young people, but note the following significant observation:

"Meanwhile, some of the factors that Church members have traditionally viewed as being important to the prevention of delinquency did not emerge as significant predictors of delinquency in this study. For instance, public religious behaviors such as attendance at church meetings and family religious behaviors such as family prayer, home evening, and family scripture study were not significantly related to lower delinquency rates among LDS youth. These activities, as important as they are to the internalization of religious values, apparently do not *in and of themselves* counteract the peer pressures to engage in unworthy behaviors. Rather, it would seem that these activities promote strength to resist temptation to the degree that they encourage our youth to pray, fast, and read the scriptures privately and help them have their own spiritual experiences" (Brent L. Top and Bruce

Chadwick, "Special Report—Teens Out of Trouble," *This People,* Fall 1995, p. 23).

We parents need to take seriously our responsibility to provide religious training in the home so that our children will in turn take religion seriously and personally. Note the following:

> As parents, we should recognize that it is important not only to hold family home evening, family prayers, and family scripture study, but also to find ways to help our children have their own personal spiritual experiences. When we hold family religious activities only to be holding them, our youth do not seem to gain the benefit needed to deter delinquency. It appears that if we are only "going through the motions," our children recognize that fact and in turn only "go through the motions" of religiosity themselves. As parents, we can demonstrate to our children that the gospel is an essential part of our lives by providing opportunities not only to learn what the gospel is, but also to experience for themselves what the gospel *does.*
>
> Similarly, it appears that local Church leaders, advisors, and teachers can best deter LDS youth from immorality, drug and alcohol abuse, and other acts of delinquency by a greater emphasis on lessons and activities that promote genuine spiritual experiences— experiences that will help the youth see Gospel principles more in practice and less in theory. We need to go beyond just expecting our youth to attend church meetings and activities to "keep them out of trouble." Activity devoid of real Gospel substance and spiritual experience does not give our youth the strength needed in this day and age to stand firm against the adversary. (Top and Chadwick, "Teens Out of Trouble," p. 24)

One of the most effective ways to gain personal spiritual experiences and testimony is to become personally involved in serving, searching, pondering, and praying.

As members of a lay church that does not have a professional, salaried clergy—a church in which people like you and me are called from the congregation to fulfill all kinds of assignments—we have a tremendous responsibility to prepare ourselves and our children. We should strive to become learned in the scriptures and doctrines, just as President Brigham Young counseled a group of elders: "There are a great many branches of education: some go to college to learn languages, some to study law, some to study physic, and some to study astronomy, and various other branches of science. . . . But our favourite study is that branch which particularly belongs to the Elders of Israel—namely, theology. Every Elder should become a profound theologian—should understand this branch better than all the world" (*Journal of Discourses,* 6:317).

This study is important not only for "the elders" but for women as well. Brigham Young has also had this statement attributed to him: "If we educate a man, we educate an individual, but if we educate a woman, we educate a family." As parents, we need to stress the importance of having our daughters as well as our sons become personally involved in learning the gospel.

An important activity for promoting gospel knowledge is to read the scriptures together daily as a family. There is real power in the scriptures. President Ezra Taft Benson said, "May I admonish you to participate in a program of daily reading and pondering of the scriptures. . . . The Book of Mormon will change your life. It will fortify you against the evils of our day. It will bring a spirituality into your life that no other book will" (*Ensign,* May 1986, p. 43).

Count the number of rich promises President Marion G. Romney made in this passage about studying the Book of Mormon: "I feel certain that if, in our homes, parents will read from the Book of Mormon prayerfully and regularly, both by themselves and with their children, the spirit of that great book will come to permeate our homes. . . . The spirit of reverence will increase; mutual respect and consideration for each other will grow. The spirit of contention will depart. Parents will counsel their children in greater love and wisdom. Children will be more responsive and submissive to the counsel of their parents. Righteousness will increase. . . . The pure love of Christ . . . will abound in our homes and lives, bringing in their wake peace, joy, and happiness" (*Ensign,* May 1980, p. 67).

We should not take those promises lightly. Obviously, we would like our children to gain a testimony that Jesus is the Christ. That knowledge is fundamental. The Book of Mormon is literally "Another Testament of Jesus Christ." Some scholars have determined that within the pages of the Book of Mormon there are 3,925 references to the Savior! No other volume is so powerfully focused on Jesus Christ. We need to emphasize the Book of Mormon in our family scripture study.

Praying, holding family home evenings, and studying the scriptures with our children are important foundations. As we strive to create a spiritual environment, our family members can be led to those experiences that will help them build their own personal testimonies.

Follow the Living Prophets

One suggestion that is as important as any other we could make is to encourage our children to tune into what the living prophets are teaching. Make a commitment as a family to follow the counsel of the living prophets. Encourage children—by teaching and example—to listen to the messages at each general conference and to reread the prophets' counsel to us from prior occasions.

About the importance of following the living prophets, President Harold B. Lee said: "We must learn to give heed to the words and commandments that the Lord shall give through his prophet, 'as if from mine own mouth, in all patience and faith.' (D&C 21:4–5.) There will be some things that take patience and faith. You may not like what comes from the authority of the Church. It may contradict your political views. It may contradict your social views. It may interfere with some of your social life. . . . Your safety and ours depends upon whether or not we follow the ones whom the Lord has placed to preside over his church" (in Conference Report, October 1970, pp. 152–53).

President Ezra Taft Benson also stressed this point: "Speaking to His prophets, the Lord said: 'He that receiveth you receiveth me' (Matthew 10:40). Always the words of the living prophet have taken precedence, for it has been God's message to the people at that particular time. Had any man accepted the ancient scripture in the days of Noah but refused to follow the revelation that Noah received and failed to board the ark, he would have been drowned. Always the words of the living prophets are of the most vital concern to the people; and always, if a man would know of Christ and learn His command-ments so that he can obey them, he must seek to find His authorized representatives" (*Teachings of Ezra Taft Benson* [Salt Lake City: Bookcraft, 1988], pp. 132–33).

Elder John A. Widtsoe felt that the very strength of the Church lies in following the living prophet. He wrote: "The most important prophet in any age is the living prophet. The prophets who have gone before have left to us their precious teachings which will be used for the instruction and comfort of mankind. But, it is the living prophet who helps us by his teachings, example, and direction to meet and to solve the problems of today, our day. To follow the living prophet, the interpreter of the past, is the essence of wisdom. The very strength of the Church lies in the doctrine of continuous revelation through a living prophet" (*Evidences and Reconciliations* [Salt Lake City: Bookcraft, 1943], p. 352).

Finally, Elder Neal A. Maxwell counseled: "Following the living prophets is something that must be done in all seasons and circumstances. We must be like President Marion G. Romney, who humbly said, '. . . I have never hesitated to follow the counsel of the Authorities of the Church even though it crossed my social, profes-sional, and political life.' (Conference Report, April 1941, p. 123.) There are, or will be, moments when prophetic declarations collide with our pride or our seeming per-sonal interests. It can happen in many ways: businessmen caught in Sunday-closing efforts who must decide how they really feel about the fourth commandment; theater owners showing near-pornographic films who must decide between prophets and profits; politicians involved in an erring movement that calls forth a First Presidency statement, forcing them to decide which flag to follow; academicians whose discipline gives rise to moral issues on which the Brethren speak out, who must choose between peers and prophets; laborers who are caught in union-shop and free-agency situations. For the participants, such painful episodes tend to force home the question: Do I believe in the living prophet even when he speaks on matters affecting me and my specialty directly? Or do I stop sustaining the prophet when his words fall in my territory? If the latter, the prophet is without honor in *our* country!" (*Things As They Really Are* [Salt Lake City: Deseret Book, 1978], p. 73).

Families can benefit greatly if they gather around at conference time and listen to the messages of the Brethren. In our own family, we have found it not only helpful but also very enjoyable to get together for a "Recap of Conference." So that the experience is fresh on our minds, we meet together on Sunday evening right after general conference has ended. This gives us a chance to have the children indicate which messages they felt were particularly helpful to them personally. Some of our most delightful and fruitful gospel discussions come out of these meetings. This practice also provides an opportunity to stress the importance of listening to and following the counsel of the living prophets.

When we look at it realistically, from both a personal and a family standpoint, we can recognize the great importance of following the words of the Brethren. Of what value is it to have living prophets if we do not heed their counsel?

Do Everything Possible to Keep Mothers with Children in the Home

Years ago, Peter Marshall, the chaplain to the United States Senate, told the story of a hermit who lived high in the mountains above a community. He was employed to care for the springs that provided water for the village below. His job was to clear the springs of debris and anything that would contaminate the water. He was called the Keeper of the Springs. One day, under a new village council, the townspeople decided they could save the salary paid to this hermit by constructing a concrete holding reservoir near the village, in which the water from the springs could be collected. They proceeded with the plan, and the employment of the Keeper of the Springs was discontinued. After a few years, moss and scum began to form in the concrete reservoir, providing a growing place for germs that caused a plague of sickness and death among the residents of the town. Soon the village leaders recognized that a great mistake had been made in not continuing the work of the Keeper of the Springs. He was reemployed, and within a few months the health of the people was restored.

The challenges of the world are real, and as parents, grandparents, and leaders, we should join in doing all we can to protect our children from the dangers around them. In order to be most helpful, we need to be sure that wherever possible we maintain the "Keepers of the Springs" in our homes.

I realize that, to some readers, the suggestion that mothers should remain at home with their children will not be pleasing. I share this idea in the hope that those mothers who *must* work outside the home will not be offended. Some mothers must earn the family's living as a result of their husbands' disabilities or physical incapacitation. Some are widows. Other mothers must assume responsibility to care for the temporal needs of their children after a divorce. These suggestions are not directed to those in such exceptional situations. However, the majority of working mothers are not in those circumstances.

We sustain the First Presidency and the Twelve as prophets, *seers,* and revelators. I sincerely feel that one of their gifts and weighty responsibilities is to see into the future and anticipate the challenges that lie ahead. They are the "watchmen on the tower" to assist us. I am convinced that their counsel to us is inspired, even though it may not be popular or palatable to many.

Years ago, the Lord's prophets began warning us of what would happen if, as a society, we did not retain the "Keepers of the Springs" in our homes and communities. Let's review together some of their counsel.

President Spencer W. Kimball said: *"Of course, there are some mothers who* must *work to support their children, and they are to be praised, not criticized,* but let every working mother honestly weigh the matter and be sure the Lord approves before she rushes her babies off to the nursery, her children off to school, her husband off to work, and herself off to her employment. Let her be certain that she is not rationalizing herself away from her children merely to provide for them greater material things. Let her analyze well before she permits her precious ones to come home to an empty house where their plaintive cry, 'Mother,' finds no loving answer" (*Faith Precedes the Miracle* [Salt Lake City: Deseret Book, 1975], p. 116; emphasis added).

President Ezra Taft Benson taught: "We need to arise and shine and to get the vision of this great work and to incorporate it into our lives and homes and our families. If we do so the Lord will bless us because He loves us. We are His people. We have accepted His gospel. You have taken upon yourselves sacred covenants and He wants to bless you. He wants to pour out His blessings, the blessings of heaven, upon you and your families. In those homes where you live the gospel, where mother and father and children are skimping just a little more to make ends meet, He will bless you even more, much more than He will *in those homes where we find so many mothers unnecessarily working outside the home in order to get better clothes, a new living room suite, a new rug on the floor. Working mothers contribute to increased divorce, to infidelity, to the weakening of homes"* (*Teachings of Ezra Taft Benson* [Salt Lake City: Bookcraft, 1988], pp. 526–27; emphasis added).

Bishop John H. Vandenberg added his thoughts: "There are further comments that advise us that economic factors indirectly play a part in the absence of parental discipline. Working mothers are not at home during most of the day, and they are unaware of what their children are doing before or after school hours or with whom they are associating. Usually when the working mother is at home, her waking hours are filled with the usual domestic chores of washing, ironing, and general household duties. The school, therefore, during five days of supervision each week, must play a serious part in teaching morality. Admittedly, this is a poor substitute for a mother's duty, and the evidence stares at us" (in Conference Report, October 1967, pp. 77–78).

Elder A. Theodore Tuttle directed these thoughts to the brethren of the Church in a general priesthood session: "I would like to say a word about working mothers, brethren. I know I am not talking to working mothers. But I am talking to some fathers whose children have working mothers. You are the ones who cause, or at least permit, mothers to work. Brethren, before you count the profit of such an endeavor, count the *cost.* In our affluent society many of us cannot distinguish between luxuries and necessities. Too often mothers work to pay for luxuries that are not worth the cost" (in Conference Report, April 1967, p. 94).

I heartily agree with Urie Bronfenbrenner's observation that every "child should spend a substantial amount of time with somebody who's crazy about him. . . . There has to be at least one person who has an irrational involvement with that child, someone who thinks that kid is more important than other people's kids, someone who's in love with him and whom he loves in return. . . . 'You can't pay a woman to do what a mother will do for free'" (*Psychology Today*, May 1977, p. 43).

We live in a time when many in the world have disparaged the role of mother and homemaker, and have taught that for "true fulfillment" a woman should not bind herself down to the mundane world of household chores and children. However, if you are a mother with children at home and you do not *have* to work away from home, I invite you to think seriously about the counsel of the prophets discussed here. Consider sincerely the importance of maintaining the "Keeper of the Springs" in your home environment, so that your family can benefit most from what you as a mother can uniquely provide.

Part Two: Summary

Ours is an exciting and challenging time in which to live. Our families need all the strength we can offer them, and the suggestions we have discussed in this section can help provide that strength. Obviously, these suggestions are not all-inclusive; add other ideas and emphases you feel would be helpful. But these provide a good starting point for your consideration:

1. Do not underestimate the power of evil.

2. Set clear moral standards and guidelines.

3. Teach your children to work.

4. Create an environment in which spiritual experiences can occur.

5. Follow the living prophets.

6. Do everything possible to keep mothers with children in the home.

As fathers and mothers, we should recognize that it is never too late to change. There is always hope. Through our efforts in working with our children and applying the principles of the gospel, we can make much progress. Consistent with the Lord's Intercessory Prayer, the intent is not to take our children out of the world but to keep them from evil. (See John 17:15.) Even if we are just beginning today, we can help our children survive spiritually and morally in a world where the pollution index continues to spiral upward.

PART THREE

Building a Better You

Among all the people—young and old—I have known over the years, I have not met one who did not want to improve in some way. Every one of us has that desire. As members of The Church of Jesus Christ of Latter-day Saints, most of us are familiar enough with the principles of the gospel to realize that if we applied those principles more fully in our lives, we would be happier and more successful. In all probability, we know more about what we ought to do than we actually put into practice. Right?

Our situation may be a little like that of the farmer who was showing a young county farm agent around his place. The agent, anxious to show off his college training, said, "Sam, you know that now we use something called contour plowing." He went on to expound on the virtues of crop rotation and hybrid strains of grain. About the time he got to the benefits of milking the cows three times a day rather than two, the old farmer said, "Hey, sonny, just a minute. I'm not farming half as well as I know how already."

Isn't that the way life is? We rarely—if ever—perform to the level of our knowledge, because it is hard to farm, or perform, as well as we know we should. To improve, we need to make genuine resolutions.

Let's consider resolutions—resolutions that can align our actions more closely with our knowledge about the gospel. You may be among those who every year make a bundle of New Year's resolutions—or maybe you have given up making resolutions because of problems you have had in keeping them. We shouldn't overlook the power of good resolutions to help make our lives happier and more successful—regardless of what we may or may not have accomplished in the past.

Let's explore for a moment the term *resolution*. As a noun, it suggests steadfastness of purpose. As an adjective, *resolute*, it is characterized by firmness or determination. As a verb, *resolve* brings to mind such things as courage, mettle, fortitude, tenacity, backbone, and moral stamina in the face of hardship, temptations, and unfavorable odds.

In the Sermon on the Mount, the Savior said, "Be ye therefore perfect, even as your Father which is in heaven is perfect" (Matthew 5:48). In the Joseph Smith Translation, we read: "Ye are therefore commanded to be perfect" (JST, Matthew 5:50). The translation of the Greek word for *perfect* means "complete, finished, fully developed." Some biblical analysts indicate that the suggestion to become perfect is exaggerated idealism or scriptural hyperbole (embellishment, enhancement, or exaggeration). As Latter-day Saints, we interpret that verse very differently.

In fact, Latter-day Saints have been criticized for believing that the Savior really meant what he said, and that becoming like our Father in Heaven and the Savior is a commandment—not just a suggestion. Over the years, many vindictive books and articles have been written condemning our beliefs as blasphemous. How dare we believe that we could and even should try to become like our Father in Heaven!

We are attacked for these beliefs even though the Bible, which is accepted as scripture by all Christians, makes frequent reference to the fact that we are children of and should become like our Father in Heaven. Note the following small sampling of the many biblical scriptures on the topic:

"What is man, that thou art mindful of him? and the son of man, that thou visitest him? For thou hast made him a little lower than the angels, and hast crowned him with glory and honour" (Psalm 8:4–5).

"I have said, *Ye are gods; and all of you are children of the most High*" (Psalm 82:6; emphasis added). The Savior even referred to this idea: "Jesus answered them, Is it not written in your law, I said, Ye are gods?" (John 10:34).

"Forasmuch then as we are the *offspring of God*, we ought not to think that the Godhead is like unto gold, or silver, or stone, graven by art and man's device" (Acts 17:29; emphasis added).

"And *if children, then heirs; heirs of God, and joint-heirs with Christ*; if so be that we suffer with him, that we may be also glorified together" (Romans 8:17; emphasis added).

"Wherefore thou art no more a servant, but *a son; and if a son, then an heir* of God through Christ" (Galatians 4:7; emphasis added).

"Furthermore we have had fathers of our flesh which corrected us, and we gave them reverence: *shall we not much rather be in subjection unto the Father of spirits, and live?* (Hebrews 12:9; emphasis added).

"Beloved, *now are we the sons of God*, and it doth not yet appear what we shall be: but we know that, *when he shall appear, we shall be like him*; for we shall see him as he is" (1 John 3:2; emphasis added).

Almost thirty years ago, Barbara and I had the opportunity of participating in a Religion in Life Conference at a southwestern university, at which I had been invited to represent a Latter-day Saint point of view. Our three days there were very busy. Among the many presentations was one I was to give to an evening philosophy class that met for two hours in an amphitheater-like lecture room with a long laboratory table stretched across the front. I had no idea who the teacher was or what his attitude might be toward institutionalized religion.

We arrived with our returned-missionary student host a few minutes before the class was to begin. The professor met us outside the door and said, basically, "Now, when you get in there, I don't want you to take the time telling the students about all the ways your church is like other churches. I want you to take the first hour and a half telling them how your church is different from other Christian churches." Then he added, with a twinkle in his eye, "And I want you to tell them in such a way that you will make Mormons out of all of them!" I interpreted this to mean that I was to speak from my heart and not hesitate to tell them what I believed.

He opened the door and ushered us into the classroom, where about eighty-five students were seated. I was hurriedly outlining in my mind some of the ideas that set our faith apart from traditional Christian faiths. (If you had received that assignment, what would you have included?)

During the next hour and a half, I shared with them some of the great distinctive ideas we have received in the doctrine and theology of the Church as restored through the Prophet Joseph Smith, including such concepts as the nature of God, the nature of man, our relationship to our Father in Heaven and Jesus Christ, the Creation, the problem of evil, continuous revelation, a lay priesthood, and eternal progression.

Then followed about thirty minutes of sincere, searching questions and responses, and the class ended. I stood at the end of the laboratory table near the exit and was speaking with a few students who wanted to ask additional questions. After a few minutes, the professor approached me and, pointing to our returned-missionary student host, said, "That fellow over there said you believe this." He had written in shorthand some notes on a pad and slowly read through them: " 'As man is, God once was, and as God is, man may become.' Do you believe that?"

I had purposely *not* used that statement during my remarks to the class, because I felt that I could raise more dust with that one than I would be able to settle in one class period. I didn't have any idea whether the professor thought the idea was good, bad, or indifferent. I explained that the statement came from Lorenzo Snow in the 1830s and was approved by the Prophet Joseph Smith. I explained that, through scripture and latter-day revelation, we have learned a lot more about what God is like. Wondering what he was thinking, and not knowing what his reaction might be to the idea, I found myself circumlocuting around and around the question, until finally I looked him squarely in the eye and simply said, "Yes, we believe that."

He looked down at his notes and slowly and thoughtfully mumbled through the words again: " 'As man is, God once was, and as God is, man may become.' Hmmmm . . . " Then, with genuine enthusiasm, he said, "That is the *greatest* idea I have ever heard!"

He was elated. He made his living by teaching ideas, and the greatest idea he had ever heard came through the Prophet Joseph Smith. Truly it is one of the most powerful beliefs we have. As believers in the restored gospel of Jesus Christ, we should take seriously the commandment, "Be ye therefore perfect," and strive continually to become more like our Father in Heaven and Jesus Christ.

There is only one verse of scripture in the entire New Testament that tells us what the Savior did to develop himself during the span of years from age twelve until he began his formal ministry at age thirty. The verse consists of just fourteen words. Count them: "And Jesus increased in wisdom and stature, and in favour with God and man" (Luke 2:52).

Developing in these four areas of our lives—the intellectual, physical, spiritual, and social—is a need many of us feel. Consider the results of an informal survey taken of 150 young adults. They were asked to list three resolutions they felt would help them become more successful and happy. Almost everyone who was surveyed (98 percent) included a resolution to increase the level of his or her spirituality. Two out of three (68 percent) indicated that they would like to improve their social skills. Half (49 percent) indicated a desire to increase their level of physical fitness, and half (48 percent) wanted to grow intellectually. The group indicated a desire to improve in the same facets of life in which the Lord grew. After all, self-improvement is at the heart of why we are here in mortality.

Let's consider some suggestions for resolutions that will help us become stronger intellectually, physically, socially, and spiritually. If we make *and keep* resolutions in these areas, we will have greater happiness and success for the rest of our lives.

Resolve to Expand Your Intellectual Horizons

Years ago, I became friends with a minister who worked with the students of his Protestant faith attending the University of Utah, where I was assigned to work with Latter-day Saint students. We knew each other on a first-name basis and often talked about our respective theological positions on a variety of issues.

One day he said, "Joe, in your church you don't have a *learned* clergy, do you?" Frankly, I didn't know whether he might have heard some bishop end a sentence with a preposition or what, but I assumed that he was referring to the basic lay nature of positions in the Church. So I responded, "You're right, Stan. The Church of Jesus Christ of Latter-day Saints is a lay church. We don't have a professional, theologically trained and salaried clergy. The leadership comes from among the regular members, who serve on a part-time basis without monetary compensation. Frankly, we feel that the Church in the Savior's time was also a lay church. Remember that Jesus called his original twelve apostles not from among the scribes, Pharisees, or Sadducees—the theologians of the day—but rather from among fishermen and tax collectors and other men making their living in a variety of vocations.

111

Nevertheless, even though we have a lay leadership within the Church, we believe that the members should become as prepared, or learned, as possible."

In terms of learning, the scriptural counsel to us is: "Seek ye out of the *best* books words of wisdom," and, " . . . become acquainted with all *good* books, and with languages, tongues, and people" (D&C 88:118; 90:15; emphasis added).

Notice the emphasis on *best* books and *good* books. What we choose to read will make a huge difference in the development of our mind and character. Obviously, the "best" books are the scriptures. They must not be overlooked, but for now let's consider good books in general.

The Lord through the Prophet Joseph Smith has counseled us to learn from a wide curriculum. Read the following scripture carefully and note the multitude of areas in which we are commanded to study: "And I give unto you a *commandment* that you shall teach one another the doctrine of the kingdom. Teach ye diligently and my grace shall attend you, that you may be instructed more perfectly in theory, in principle, in doctrine, in the law of the gospel, in all things that pertain unto the kingdom of God, that are expedient for you to understand; of things both in heaven and in the earth, and under the earth [subjects such as astronomy and geology]; things which have been [history], things which are [current events], things which must shortly come to pass; things which are at home, things which are abroad [domestic and international issues and events]; the wars and the perplexities of the nations [political science], and the judgments which are on the land; and a knowledge also of countries and of kingdoms [geography and on and on]" (D&C 88:77–79; emphasis added).

It is certainly clear that as members of this lay church, with no professionally trained and salaried ministers, we are definitely expected to become learned! We should strive diligently to become knowledgeable—not only about scriptures and doctrine but in a host of other areas as well.

Decide now that you will commit yourself to read good books—not just when you are involved in a formal university or school course, but throughout your life. A few years ago, a disturbing poll indicated that more than half the college graduates in the study never completely read a serious book following their graduation. Contrast that with the attitude of one of my university classmates, who said to me on the day we were graduated, "Joe, now that we have the degree, we are free to read the books we really want to read." He has gone on expanding his background and generally increasing in learning.

At some point in our lives, we learned to read. The question we should ask ourselves is: Are we reading now? Are we actually growing in wisdom? Are we overcoming the tendency of our populace to be simply a visually learning people—depending mainly on television?

We cannot justify mentally shifting into neutral and failing to exert our efforts to make progress intellectually. Back in 1838, Sidney Rigdon, a member of the First Presidency, addressed a group of relatively new members of the Church, some of whom apparently thought that all they had to do was to have faith in Christ, repent of their sins, be baptized, receive the gift of the Holy Ghost, and then just sit back and wait to receive the celestial glory. He said: "Vain are the hopes of those who embrace the gospel, and then suppose . . . they have nothing more to do. . . . The great God . . . never thought of . . . raising up a society of ignoramuses, but men and women of . . . intelligence as high as human nature was susceptible" (*Elder's Journal* 1 [August 1838]: 53).

So whether or not you are in a formal educational setting, the challenge is the same: Continue learning throughout your entire life.

Rufus Choate said, "Happy is he who has laid up in his youth, and held fast in all fortune, a genuine and passionate love for reading." In this area, my father-in-law was a real inspiration to me. He was the twelfth of thirteen children of a very poor convert immigrant family from Switzerland. After he had finished the first six years of elementary school, he, like many others in his time, was encouraged to drop out and learn a trade. Then one day he met Mr. Hicks, the new schoolteacher in Midway, Utah. Mr. Hicks asked, "Albert, are you coming to school this year?" Albert explained that he was not planning to come back to school. Mr. Hicks said, "Well, why don't you come for three or four days and see how you like it?"

Albert came, and his future life was dramatically changed for the better. He said that this new teacher didn't just answer the questions that were raised in class, but he wrote on the chalkboard the titles of books in which the students could find the answers. Albert developed a thirst for learning that was never quenched.

Albert Kohler was a hard-working farmer providing for a large family, but I hardly remember his ever being in the house without having a book—a thick book—in his work-worn hands. He would circle words he didn't know and write their definitions in the margins. He was a real student of history as well as of the doctrine of the Church. I remember the first gift we gave him after we were married: William Prescott's *The Conquest of Mexico and Peru.* He read the entire book carefully. Although he never had the opportunity to go beyond the eighth grade, he read much more than most college graduates. He not only learned to read, he read.

Walter B. Pitkin said, "Even with all the leisure in the world and an income large enough to gratify all desires, men will seldom read serious books at the rate of twenty a year." Now, just imagine that you were to read an entire book each week for the next fifty years. You would read more than 2,500 books. That might seem like a lot of reading. However, there are reportedly in the Library of Congress today more than 27,000,000 volumes! In addition, it is estimated that books are rolling off the presses of the world at the rate of a thousand titles per day. That means that in fifty years there will be more than 18,000,000 additional volumes! If you were to read continuously, you would not be able to read more than a tiny fraction of the books already in print, let alone those that are appearing on the shelves every day. Consequently, and here is the point, *we should not waste a minute—even a minute—reading anything but that which is uplifting and instructive.*

There is a lot of frivolous, useless, and morally destructive literature in print that falls far short of the category of "best books." Paxton Hood said, "Be as careful of the books you read as of the company you keep; for your habits and character will be as much influenced by the former as by the latter."

Here is a practical suggestion that I have found helpful: Ask a few respected people of high character—those you know read a lot—to share with you the titles of the five books (besides the scriptures) that they feel have had the most positive influence in shaping their lives for the better. You will soon accumulate a good list of titles to add to those you have already decided to read. This idea corresponds to a suggestion made by Emerson, "If we encountered a man of rare intellect we should ask him what books he read." Then I would add, if we follow the example of wise people who are readers, we will grow in wisdom. We will become more *interested* in life as well as more *interesting* to others.

In addition to resolving that we will read only the best in print, it would be *very* beneficial to our spirits if we resolved not to watch even one R-rated or X-rated (NC-17) movie, video, or television show from now on. That may appear to some to be an extreme position, but I assure you that much of our future happiness and success depends on it.

In this area as in others, there is safety in following the living prophets. President Ezra Taft Benson said: "Consider carefully the words of the prophet Alma to his errant (and promiscuous) son, Corianton, 'Forsake your sins, and go no more after the lusts of your eyes.' (Alma 39:9.) 'The lusts of your eyes.' In our day, what does that expression mean? Movies, television programs, and video recordings that are both suggestive and lewd. Magazines and books that are obscene and pornographic. We counsel you . . . not to pollute your minds with such degrading matter, for the mind through which this filth passes is never the same afterwards. Don't see R-rated movies or vulgar videos or participate in any entertainment that is immoral, suggestive, or pornographic" (*Ensign,* May 1986, p. 45). Filling our minds with this kind of trash is one of the most effective tools Satan has to pacify and lull us into carnal security, cheat our souls, and lead us carefully down to hell (see 2 Nephi 28:21).

There are literally "evils and designs which do and will exist in the hearts of conspiring men in the last days" (D&C 89:4), and almost anything will be offered if there is a profit to be made. Some of the finest people I know have become addicted to the pornographic sleaze that surrounds us, and they have experienced serious personal and family problems as a result. Some have fallen into immoral paths and have actually lost their membership in the Church.

In addition to the problems presented by the sexually inappropriate and all-too-explicit content seen on television and in the movies, with the advancement of technology we are faced with serious challenges on the electronic highway. Now, all who subscribe can literally have access to anything they choose, and thus the worst forms of pornography are verbally and graphically portrayed.

Recently, James, a young attorney, called us. He was obviously very upset. He said, "I can't believe it. Emily has sued me for a divorce. It seems impossible . . . and after only two years! I had noticed that not long ago she started to act a little different, but I didn't think much about it. Since then, she has confessed that she became acquainted with this guy through her computer on the Internet. They 'visited' several times, exchanging messages, and finally arranged to meet one night after she got off work. Then it happened. I guess she will probably be excommunicated."

Reasons abound for us to be careful about what we choose to see or do with the media. Books, television, movies, electronic data—a huge variety of information is available to us. If we follow the counsel of the prophets and choose "out of the best," we can grow intellectually and continue learning throughout our lives.

IDEA 2

Resolve to Preserve and Strengthen Your Physical Body

More than 160 years ago, in 1833, the Lord revealed through the Prophet Joseph Smith an impressive health code that we call the Word of Wisdom. In those years not much was known or taught about good nutrition, but since that time science has progressively discovered that the truths taught in the Word of Wisdom were indeed inspired. In 1988, the surgeon general of the United States indicated that 68 percent of all the deaths in the United States are related to diet (see Kenneth E. Johnson, M.D., *Mormon Wisdom and Health* [Cedar Fort, Utah: Cedar Fort, Inc., 1993], p. xiv). Following the counsel contained in the Word of Wisdom can make all the difference in how we feel and perform physically. With good health, we can be happier and more successful. Without it, we are curtailed in almost every other way.

Among the "do's" and "don'ts" in the Word of Wisdom are the following:

"Inasmuch as any man drinketh wine or strong drink among you, behold it is not good . . . again, strong drinks are not for the belly. . . .

"Tobacco is not for the body . . . and is not good for man. . . .

"Hot drinks are not for the body." (This verse was interpreted early on as referring to coffee and tea, the "hot drinks" of the day. In addition to the harmful stimulants contained in these beverages, a competent dentist told me that great damage is done to the sensitive tissues of the mouth and throat by the hot temperature as well. So the next time you see someone carefully clasping and slurping a steaming cup of coffee, know that he is doing harm to his system in more ways than one.)

"All wholesome herbs God hath ordained for the constitution, nature, and use of man—

"Every herb in the season thereof, and every fruit in the season thereof. . . .

"Flesh also of beasts and of the fowls . . . are to be used sparingly; and . . . only in times of winter, or of cold, or famine.

"All grain is ordained for the use of man . . . to be the staff of life. . . . Nevertheless, wheat for man" (D&C 89:5–17).

Then this remarkable promise is given: "And all saints who remember to keep and do these sayings, walking in obedience to the commandments, shall receive health in their navel and marrow to their bones; and shall find wisdom and great treasures of knowledge, even hidden treasures; and shall run and not be weary, and shall walk and not faint. And I, the Lord, give unto them a promise, that the destroying angel shall pass by them, as the children of Israel, and not slay them" (D&C 89:18–21).

In the previous chapter, we considered the importance of growing intellectually. Note that included within these remarkable promises of the Word of Wisdom is a direct covenant that if we follow the counsel, we will find "wisdom and great treasures of knowledge."

What a blessing it would be if each of us determined

that from this time on we would receive appropriate nutrition, as counseled in the Word of Wisdom, and also adequate rest and exercise. Let's briefly consider each of these three vital areas in a little more detail. They all play a role in helping us preserve and strengthen our physical health so that we can "grow in stature" as we should.

Resolve to get an adequately balanced diet. Receiving proper nutrition is an area in which it is hard for many of us to perform up to the level of our knowledge. We live in a time when much is being said but often little is done in regards to eating a balanced and healthy diet. Some have even come to call it the "cholesterol" age.

In a generation of fast and fatty foods, many young people have grown up without the emphasis they need in the area of diet. A tongue-in-cheek incident illustrates the point: A friend of ours, Petrea Kelly, was giving her son that final parental review that most missionaries get prior to entering the door of the Missionary Training Center.

The mother said, "Now, Bronson, you have your toothbrush and your pajamas?"

"Yes, Mom," he answered patiently.

"You remember how to iron a shirt, and be sure to put a cloth between the iron and your suit pants when you press them."

"Yes, Mom! But we'd better hurry, we're going to be late."

"Okay, Son. Before we leave, just repeat back to me the four basic food groups."

"Sure, Mom," he said. "The four basic food groups for a prospective missionary are: peanut butter, Hostess chocolate cupcakes and Twinkies, chocolate milk, and ramen noodles."

For some young people, when it comes to diet, there may be more truth than humor in that exchange. If this young man had continued with that philosophy on food, he could have ended up like another good friend of ours whose wife had been encouraging him to take off some weight. She said, "Bill, there are fifty pounds of you that I am not sealed to."

We should firmly resolve that in addition to avoiding the "don'ts" in the Word of Wisdom, we will follow the "do's." How often today we read that we should eat plenty of fresh fruits, vegetables, and whole grains. Now, in many of the publications and counsels from nutritional experts, we see a redrafting of the traditional basic foods charts to appear as though the Prophet Joseph Smith might have drafted them along the lines of the Word of Wisdom that he received by inspiration back in 1833!

With increasing frequency, authorities are discovering that diet affects the way we feel, how we look, how we develop physically ("grow in stature"), how our minds and nervous systems operate, and even how we show signs of aging. If we are serious about utilizing diet to improve our physical health and thus increase our chances for success and happiness, we should remember and apply the following counsel: Emphasize whole grains, legumes (beans), potatoes, corn, brown rice, fresh vegetables (especially the green ones), and fresh fruits.

We are told to eat meat sparingly, and yet if you were to ask anyone what they would serve company for dinner, they would probably say something like, "Oh, we plan to have roast beef (or steak or shrimp or some other meat dish)." Generally speaking, we eat meat—too much and too often.

We can learn that a meal does not have to feature a meat dish every time in order to be enjoyable. We would probably do well if we used meat more like they do in Asian countries, as a garnish or flavoring. In addition to improving our health, such a habit would benefit our budget. It really would be a "win-win" situation.

Then, of course, we should resolve to avoid *completely*

the "don'ts" in the Word of Wisdom, including tobacco in all its forms, alcohol, addictive stimulants, coffee, tea, and illegal drugs of any type. If any of these negative practices have been or are a part of your life, resolve right now, at this very moment, that from now on you will absolutely not participate in the "don'ts"—*ever!*

I remember a young man I'll call George, who had one of the brightest minds I've ever known, especially in the areas of mathematics and science. He almost always had his hand in the air, signaling his desire to answer the teacher's questions. His bedtime reading selections were often volumes of the family's set of encyclopedias. When George got to high school, he unfortunately fell into the wrong company—the group that cut classes and congregated down in the basement by the lockers or across the street from the school. They began to experiment with tobacco, then marijuana, on to cocaine, LSD, and even heroine. George got in all kinds of trouble and has been in and out of prison on a variety of charges and received treatment at the state mental institution. At this point, his mind has been so affected that it is difficult for him to have enough coordination to even turn a doorknob without difficulty. A brilliant mind was virtually destroyed because he failed to follow the simple and wise counsel in the Word of Wisdom.

What an improved situation we would live in if only the whole world would resolve to accept the Word of Wisdom! We would see fewer heart and lung diseases, a reduction in the number of broken homes and other associated costs of alcoholism, a decrease in violence and the problems associated with illegal drugs, and consequently a decline in social diseases. Literally billions of dollars and thousands of lives would be saved.

Resolve to get adequate physical exercise. We are counseled to choose some sport or other vigorous exercise that is consistent with our physical condition and be regular in pursuing it. We should get the blood circulating and give our major muscles a workout. An appropriate amount of time and effort spent in exercising will help us to be more effective in all other areas of our lives.

I don't know what your choice will be. Personally, I prefer playing racquetball or walking to jogging. I haven't seen many joggers who look really happy while they are doing it, although I do have friends who rarely miss their three to six miles a day. Of course, you need to make your own choice, but resolve to do something physical that you enjoy, and do it regularly. If there is any question about what exercise would be appropriate, consult with your physician or other specialists.

Barbara and I have discovered that during our early-morning walks together we receive a double benefit. We not only get some good physical exercise, but we have some time together to talk through whatever is on our minds. We solve most of the problems of the world on those walks.

It is easy to rationalize that we don't have time to exercise. Not so. Ultimately, our improved health through exercise will provide us more time and energy to accomplish other tasks. We can usually do about whatever we want to—if we want to badly enough.

Resolve to get adequate rest. In the area of rest, the counsel from the Lord is very clear: "Cease to sleep longer than is needful; retire to thy bed early, that ye may not be weary; arise early, that your bodies and your minds may be invigorated" (D&C 88:124).

Some people do not get the rest they need. Others become habituated to going to bed late and then sleeping much longer than their systems really need. Thus they miss out on some of the personal inspiration they desperately need and could be receiving. In the area of personal inspiration, as the prophets have said, "We live far beneath our privileges."

Years ago, Barbara and I had a special opportunity to chauffeur President and Sister Marion G. Romney from Provo to their home in Salt Lake City. Along the way, President Romney shared some of his personal experiences from when he was first called to serve as a General Authority in 1941. He had been serving as a stake president at the time, and had gone to general conference. To his amazement, he was announced and sustained as a new General Authority—an Assistant to the Quorum of the Twelve—without his prior knowledge; no one had talked to him about the calling before the session started. He was shocked and very nervous. He felt that he needed some advice, and so he went to Elder Harold B. Lee, a relatively new member of the Quorum of the Twelve and a former contemporary as a stake president. Elder Romney asked him for advice about how to be successful as a General Authority.

Elder Lee spoke about the necessity of receiving personal revelation in order to be effective and said: "If you are to be successful as a General Authority, you will need to be inspired. You will need to receive revelation. I will give you *one* piece of advice: *Go to bed early and get up early.* If you do, your body and mind will become rested and then in the quiet of those early morning hours, you will receive more flashes of inspiration and insight than at any other time of the day."

President Romney said: "From that day on, I put that counsel into practice, and I know it works. Whenever I have a serious problem, or some assignment of a creative nature with which I hope to receive the influence of the Spirit, I always receive more assistance in the early morning hours than at any other time of the day. Following that counsel has helped me a great deal through the years."

You can have a similar experience in your own life. You can change, even if you consider yourself a "night person." I remember a conversation with a young elder at the Missionary Training Center. On the first day he was there, he mentioned, "President, I don't know about going to bed around ten and getting up at six in the morning. You see, I'm a 'night person.' I don't go to bed that early. I usually don't get creative until about midnight or one o'clock in the morning." I assured him, "Elder, if you will get up in the morning at 6:00 A.M. sharp and go through the ten hours of classroom instruction, get a good workout in your gym class, and do all the other things on the schedule, come bedtime, you will be able to go to sleep."

Before his time at the MTC had ended, he had made the adjustment.

It has been said that almost any habit—good or bad— can be set in about twenty-one days. With firm resolve, we can make the needed changes in our lives. If we provide the needed care for our physical bodies, we will have the strength to grow and serve the Lord in other areas of our lives.

Resolve to Be a Truer Friend

The philosopher Aristotle said: "In poverty and other misfortunes of life, true friends are a sure refuge. The young they keep out of mischief; to the old they are a comfort and aid in their weakness, and those in the prime of life they incite to noble deeds."

Even after a couple is married, it is a blessing to have good friends, even though the list may be quite different from the friends each of the spouses had when single. A friend of ours told us: "My list of friends has changed a great deal over the years. Although I have nothing against any of the friends I knew in high school, our lives have moved in different directions and so there really isn't much contact at all now. Even though I still feel close to a few former roommates and friends I had at college, the best friends we now have are those we have met together, with whom we have a lot in common. Some we've met at church, and others, in the neighborhood. It's kind of like Jim had his friends and I had mine before we were married, but the ones we prize the most are those we have come to know together. Associating with them brings Jim and me closer together."

The need for a couple to develop new friends together is illustrated by Natalie, who described her situation this way: "Before Brent straightened out his life and became worthy for us to be married in the temple, many of his best friends were not living up to the standards of the Church. One of my major worries is that he will someday get involved again with the same group and slip back into his old habits. That really could wreck our marriage."

Natalie's fears are not unreasonable. Ann tells of how her husband's friends and their activities are threatening her marriage. "He comes home from work, cleans up, eats dinner, and goes off with his friends golfing, playing ball, or going into the mountains for one reason or another. I hardly have a chance to have a conversation with him before he is on his way. I definitely feel like I take a distant second place to his friends." It is appropriate to allow some space for each partner in a marriage to pursue individual interests with friends, but if that is overdone it places too much strain on the marriage.

Some get too heavily involved in television or athletic events, affecting the quality of their marriages by spending a disproportionate amount of time with those "friends." One wife took the time to cross-stitch this message, which she hung in a prominent place in their family room: "We interrupt this marriage to bring you the football season."

Cultivating appropriate friendship, though, is a very important ingredient in enriching a marriage. As Ralph Waldo Emerson said, "We take care of our health, we lay up money, we make our roof tight and our clothing sufficient, but who provides wisely that he shall not be wanting in the best property of all—friends." Some choose to travel with friends. Some enjoy annual camp-outs in scenic venues; others have study groups and book clubs where they discuss uplifting topics of mutual interest. Time spent in this way can really be an investment in making life more interesting.

If our friendships are to be enriching, we need to be the

kind of people with whom others of high standards would enjoy associating. Weir Mitchell said, "He alone has lost the art to live who cannot win new friends." Because almost all of us would like to have more friends, let's consider what we can do to develop the capacity to cultivate them.

More than fifty years ago, Dale Carnegie wrote *How to Win Friends and Influence People.* Over fifty million copies are now in print. In this fine book he listed some time-honored principles for making friends, suggestions that are just as valuable today as they were half a century ago. Among them are:

Become genuinely interested in other people.

Smile. (Remember, the Lord *commanded* us to "be of good cheer.")

Remember that a person's name is to that person the sweetest and most important sound in any language.

Be a good listener. Encourage others to talk about themselves.

Talk in terms of the other person's interests.

Make the other person feel important—and do it sincerely. (See Dale Carnegie, *How to Win Friends and Influence People* [New York: Simon & Schuster, 1936], p. 112.)

I doubt that my mother ever read Carnegie's book, but she had a phenomenal capacity to make friends. His principles seemed almost instinctive in her. She really applied that universal "new commandment" the Lord gave us to love one another. It didn't matter to her what a person's station in life was—her capacity to love was broad and genuine.

I remember one day when Dad and I had gone to Preston to buy some replacement parts for our broken-down wheat harvester. We were in our Ford pickup truck making the ten-mile trip back to the field. Just as we got to the outskirts of town, we passed two hitchhikers. They were unshaven and looked pretty rough to us—like maybe they had slept all night in a coal car or something. We passed them by.

Later, when we went into the house for lunch, Mom told us about having gone to Preston in the family car to do some grocery shopping. "When I was leaving town," she said, "I saw these two poor men standing at the side of the road hitchhiking. They looked hungry to me and like they really needed some help, so I picked them up and gave them a ride out to Marion's (a small combination gas station and grocery store). I told Marion to give them what they needed to eat and let me know what the charges were so that I could take care of the bill."

I glanced out of the corner of my eye at Dad.

Of course, picking up strangers on the highway these days would be much more risky and generally not recommended. But on that occasion, I think both Dad and I recognized that somehow we had been outdone. Mom was always concerned for the needs of others. She had a remarkable capacity to make friends with people of all ages and circumstances.

Let's consider next our personal appearance. Some people are overly concerned with how they look and how they dress. Some fall into serious problems by spending far too much of their family's money on "costly apparel." At least ten times in the Book of Mormon, "costly apparel" is mentioned as having contributed to the downfall of a society. For example:

"And it came to pass in the eighth year of the reign of the judges, that the people of the church began to wax proud, because of their exceeding riches, *and their fine silks, and their fine-twined linen,* and because of their many flocks and herds, and their gold and their silver, and all manner of precious things, which they had obtained by their industry; and in all these things were they lifted up in the pride of their eyes, for they began to wear very costly apparel" (Alma 4:6; emphasis added).

"And now my beloved brethren, I say unto you, can ye withstand these sayings; yea, can ye lay aside these things, and trample the Holy One under your feet; yea, can ye be puffed up in the pride of your hearts; yea, *will ye still persist in the wearing of costly apparel* and setting your hearts upon the vain things of the world, upon your riches?" (Alma 5:53; emphasis added).

After the Nephites had lived in peace and harmony for more than two hundred years, "there began to be among them those who were *lifted up in pride, such as the wearing of costly apparel,* and all manner of fine pearls, and of the fine things of the world" (4 Nephi 1:24; emphasis added).

Nevertheless, our personal appearance should not be unduly neglected. One of my friends mentioned: "Before we were married, Debra always looked so sharp. She was concerned with how her hair was fixed and what she wore. Now, at almost any time of the day, she really looks like she doesn't care about how she looks, and it bothers me. Do you have any recommendations?"

It is true that before marriage most of us are concerned about how we look and the impression we make on others. Sometimes, after we are married, we become careless. It would be good for each of us occasionally to look long and hard in a full-length mirror. Certainly we should not become too obsessed with how we look, but we should work to improve our physical appearance as much as would be reasonable.

President Spencer W. Kimball said: "How nice and easy would it be if we had a magic wand! But we haven't. You might take a careful inventory of your habits, your speech, your appearance, your weight, . . . and your eccentricities. . . . Take each item and analyze it. What do you like in others? What personality traits please you in others? Are your dresses too short, too long, too revealing, too old-fashioned? Does your weight drive off possible suitors? Do you laugh raucously? Are you too selfish? Are you interested only in your own interests?" (*Teachings of Spencer W. Kimball* [Salt Lake City: Bookcraft, 1982], pp. 295–96).

The Lord expects us to do the best we can with what he has given us. Speaking about improving appearance, President David O. McKay reportedly said, "Even a barn looks better when it's painted." After we have done what we can to improve how we look, it's then time to forget about ourselves and spend our time thinking of others and their needs. In this way, we can cultivate friendships more easily while at the same time deepening the friendship we each should have with our spouse.

When my brother-in-law came home from his mission and started to think more seriously about whom he would marry, he told his mother, "You know, Mom, what I need to find is a girl to marry who is really smarter than the average, has a good figure, and is athletic, healthy, and really socially on top of things." His mother responded, "Have you thought about what you need to do in order to merit a girl like that? You need to think more about developing in yourself all the qualities you are hoping to find in someone else." That is good counsel not only before but after marriage.

If we work harder to *be* "Mr. Right" or "Mrs. Right," we will more likely have the marriage we desire. May the Lord bless us all to be able to cultivate good friends, and in the end to feel that we have married our best friend.

IDEA 4

Resolve to Overcome Inappropriate Human Pride

If we are to increase in "favor with God," we must resolve to overcome as much as possible the sin of inappropriate human pride. President Ezra Taft Benson called pride the universal sin and "the great stumbling block to Zion." He said:

> Most of us think of pride as self-centeredness, conceit, boastfulness, arrogance, or haughtiness. All of these are elements of the sin, but the heart, or core, is still missing. The central feature of pride is enmity—enmity toward God and enmity toward our fellowmen. . . .
>
> Pride is a sin that can readily be seen in others but is rarely admitted in ourselves. Most of us consider pride to be a sin of those on the top, such as the rich and the learned, looking down at the rest of us. (See 2 Ne. 9:42.) There is, however, a far more common ailment among us—and that is pride from the bottom looking up. It is manifest in so many ways, such as faultfinding, gossiping, backbiting, murmuring, living beyond our means, envying, coveting, withholding

gratitude and praise that might lift another, and being unforgiving and jealous. (*Ensign,* May 1989, pp. 4–5)

We would all be blessed by reading or rereading President Benson's entire sermon—it is one of the classics on the subject of pride.

C. S. Lewis also recognized the serious nature of pride. He wrote that pride is the "parent" sin and leads to every other evil. As he put it: "The essential vice, the utmost evil, is Pride. Unchastity, anger, greed, drunkenness, and all that are mere fleabites in comparison: it was through Pride that the devil became the devil: Pride leads to every other vice: it is the complete anti-God state of mind. Does this seem to you exaggerated? If so, think it over. . . . The more pride one had, the more one disliked pride in others. In fact, if you want to find out how proud you are the easiest way is to ask yourself, 'How much do I dislike it when other people snub me, or refuse to take any notice of me, or shove their oar in or patronize me, or show off?' The point is that each person's pride is in competition with every one else's pride. . . . Pride is essentially competitive. . . . Pride gets no pleasure out of having something, only in having more of it than the next man. . . . Nearly all those evils in the world which people put down to greed or selfishness are really far more the result of Pride" (*The Best of C. S. Lewis,* from "Mere Christianity," Christianity Today Edition [New York: Iversen Associates, 1969], pp. 497–98).

Every one of us, to one degree or another, suffers from the problem of inappropriate human pride. Not one of us is completely free from its effects, but we must do all in our power to overcome its influence if we are to grow in favor with God.

As human beings, we have a *remarkable* capacity to fall under the influence of pride—even when we think we are in the safest of religious settings. I remember reading about a Sunday School teacher who taught her class that great scriptural lesson on the proud Pharisee who had thanked the Lord that he was not a sinner like the publican, and the penitent publican who knew he was a sinner and prayed for forgiveness. Jesus said that the publican went down to his home more justified than the Pharisee. The Sunday School teacher then suggested to her class that they should all thank God that they were not like that Pharisee! Even in the best of settings, pride creeps up on us.

If we are not careful, we could even have a problem with the definite article "The" in the formal name of The Church of Jesus Christ of Latter-day Saints. We know that this is not just "a" church of Jesus Christ. This is "The" Church of Jesus Christ—"the only true and living church upon the face of the whole earth" (D&C 1:30). Our restored knowledge of such doctrines as eternal marriage, priesthood keys, and the plan of salvation gives us unique qualifications and responsibilities to teach the world. Sometimes this is interpreted as demonstrating that we think we are better than others.

Once we begin to think that belonging to "The" Church of Jesus Christ somehow makes us better than those who do not belong, we find ourselves guilty of the sin of pride. In reality, as a church, we have no monopoly on goodness. Obviously, some of the best people in the world haven't even heard of, let alone become members of, The Church of Jesus Christ of Latter-day Saints. Basically, about all we can conclude about our own personal goodness is that if we as members of the Church are living up to the standards of the gospel, we are likely better than we would otherwise have been.

Reportedly, a Carthusian monk was asked to explain to an inquirer about the distinctive features of his monastic order. He explained: "When it comes to good works, we don't match the Benedictines; as to preaching, we are not in a class with the Dominicans; the Jesuits are away ahead of us in learning; but in the matter of humility, we're tops" (adapted from Robert J. McCracken, *What Is Sin? What Is Virtue?* [New York: Harper and Row, 1966, p. 14).

Even in Church callings there can be danger. We may fall into the trap of aspiring to position. I remember an experience I had with a young missionary who had just arrived at the Missionary Training Center. He said, "President, do you know what my main goal is on my mission?" Of course I didn't know, and so I asked him. "My main goal is to become assistant to the president of my mission!" he answered. (As I remember it, *my* was a prominent word in his conversation.)

I thought to myself, What a shame! How much better it would have been for him to have said something like, "President, the main goal I have on my mission is to be a worthy representative of the Lord Jesus Christ. I want to serve him with all my heart, might, mind, and strength. I would be happy to serve in whatever part of the mission and in whatever assignment I am given. I just want to serve."

I was impressed with an experience related by President Boyd K. Packer, who told of a friend's asking him which elder in his mission was the most outstanding. As I recall, President Packer at first indicated that there had been several outstanding elders in his mission. When his friend still pressed to know which of all those notable elders was the most outstanding, he described an elder who was a good teacher of the gospel, knew the discussions well, and worked hard. Interestingly, this elder (we'll call him Elder Jones) had not held any of the positions some missionaries feel are the most important—district or zone leader or assistant to the president. He was never "more" than a senior companion. Whenever a new group of missionaries would enter the mission, President Packer would interview all the elders, select the one he felt had the most leadership potential, and assign him to work with Elder Jones. After one or two months, Elder Jones would receive another new companion, and later another, throughout his whole mission. President Packer said, "I wanted to have as many elders in the mission as near like Elder Jones as we could possibly have."

Where we serve doesn't matter nearly so much as *how* we serve. There are no unimportant assignments or callings in the Lord's Church.

We need to remember that our Savior, Redeemer, and the Creator of worlds without number—truly the greatest of all—set the example of humble service by kneeling and washing his disciples' feet. Imagine how Peter must have felt to have the Messiah kneeling at his feet to provide this humblest of services. In that era, the washing of feet was a common practice, what with the open sandals, dusty roads, and dirty streets. It was common for an individual to wash his own feet, but not for the master of the house to provide the service. Peter knew by personal revelation received on the coasts of Caesarea Philippi (see Matthew 16:13–19) that this Jesus kneeling there was literally the Christ, the Anointed One. He asked, "Lord, dost thou wash my feet?" and later responded as I think many of us would, "Thou shalt never wash my feet." He must have felt that the situation should have been reversed. He should have been the one kneeling at the Master's feet. But Jesus said, "If I wash thee not, thou hast no part with me." Then Peter, with his characteristic enthusiasm, said, "Lord, not my feet only, but also my hands and my head." He wanted to be with the Lord all the way.

When the Savior took his place again, he asked the disciples, "Know ye what I have done to you? Ye call me Master and Lord: and ye say well; for so I am. If I then, your Lord and Master, have washed your feet; ye also ought to wash one another's feet. For I have given you an example, that ye should do as I have done to you. Verily,

verily, I say unto you, The servant is not greater than his lord; neither he that is sent greater than he that sent him" (John 13:4–16).

In contrast to such humility, pride causes us to become overly concerned, as we compare ourselves with others, about how intelligent we think we are, the brand of our jeans or other clothing—the "costly apparel" we wear, to what organizations we belong, on which side of town we live, how much money we have, what our race or nationality is, what kind of car we drive, even to what church we belong, how much education we have been privileged to acquire, and on and on and on.

In the scriptures there are many indications that pride has risen to destroy individuals, nations, and in some cases even the Church itself. Remember the plight of the Nephites:

> And they began again to prosper and to wax great. . . . And now there was nothing in all the land to hinder the people from prospering continually, except they should fall into transgression. . . .
>
> And it came to pass that there were many cities built anew, and there were many old cities repaired [a real urban renewal program].
>
> And there were many highways cast up, . . . which led from city to city, and from land to land. . . . [Some sort of an interstate highway system, I suppose.]
>
> But it came to pass . . . there began to be some disputings among the people; and *some were lifted up unto pride* and boastings because of their exceedingly great riches, yea, even unto great persecutions;
>
> For there were many merchants in the land, and also many lawyers, and many officers. [Apparently, a real stratified society developed.]
>
> And the people began to be distinguished by ranks, *according to their riches and their chances for learning;* yea, some were ignorant because of their poverty, and others did receive great learning because of their riches.

> Some were lifted up in pride. . . . And thus there
> became a great inequality in all the land, insomuch
> that the church began to be broken up. (3 Nephi
> 6:4–14; emphasis added)

It has been calculated that no fewer than thirty times
throughout the Book of Mormon the cycles of prosperity
and peace were destroyed, principally by the effects of
human pride.

Our opportunities, our relative prosperity, and our
socially stratified communities make overcoming inappropriate pride a genuine challenge. Our cup of advantages is very full and, as the English proverb states, "A full
cup must be carried steadily."

Some years ago, just after finishing graduate school, I
was visiting with an acquaintance who was much older—
probably twice my years. Earlier in his career he had gone
back East to a major university and received graduate
training from some well-known scholars in his field.

In the course of our conversation, my friend was critical of the leaders of the Church and some of the policies
that he felt should long since have been changed. Then
he said these words, which still ring in my memory, "You
see, Joe, I am an intellectual." (Frankly, in my experience,
the *genuine* intellectual does not have to announce it.)

Since that time, this brother has spent his life on the
fringe, speaking, writing, and associating with those who
feel they know more than the designated leaders of the
Church. These negative and critical attitudes have
affected his wife, some of their children, and even some
of their grandchildren. In my mind, this is the type of
individual Jacob had in mind when he warned: "O that
cunning plan of the evil one! O the vainness, and the
frailties, and the foolishness of men! *When they are learned
they think they are wise,* and they hearken not unto the
counsel of God, for they set it aside, *supposing they know*

of themselves, wherefore, *their wisdom is foolishness and it profiteth them not. And they shall perish.* But to be learned is good *if* they hearken unto the counsels of God (2 Nephi 9:28–29; emphasis added).

A young man from a small town in central Utah came to the University of Utah and soon proved himself to be a very successful student—academically, that is. John, as we'll call him, had learned the jargon related to his professional studies—as is so often the case, it was like learning a foreign language. He said, "You know, when I go back home it is really tough. Folks back there don't seem to understand what I'm talking about. They are really backward and sort of out of it." In contrast, I remember hearing my father refer to an equally highly educated individual who came back to visit my hometown of Banida, Idaho. Dad said, "You know, there is something special about him. It doesn't matter who he is with. He doesn't use fancy words. He always talks in a way that everyone can understand him." People who use their "chances for learning" as an excuse to put themselves above others are permitting themselves to be trapped by the sin of pride. We all face the same challenge, and succumbing to it could also inhibit our spiritual growth.

In conclusion, consider this insightful warning from author Robert J. McCracken: "If we make a listing of our sins, [pride] . . . is the one that heads the list, breeds all the rest, and does more to estrange us from our neighbors or from God than any evil we can commit. . . . In this aspect, it is not only the worst of the seven deadly sins; it is the parent sin, the one that leads to every other, the sin from which no one is free" (*What Is Sin? What Is Virtue?,* pp. 11–13). May we all strive to overcome the dangers of pride and walk in humility before the Lord.

Resolve to Grow Spiritually

In the informal survey mentioned in the introduction to this section, 98 percent of the respondents indicated a desire to grow spiritually. Following are several simple ideas that will make a big difference.

Resolve now that you will read from the scriptures daily. When President Ezra Taft Benson gave his first speech in general conference after he became the President of the Church, I remember how impressed I was with his emphasis on the Book of Mormon and the importance of our reading from it every day. I was thinking that at the next general conference he might speak on the importance of our reading from the other standard works. However, as you may recall, he reemphasized the importance of the Book of Mormon—as he did in succeeding conferences, again and again. The Book of Mormon really is "Another Testament of Jesus Christ."

If you started on the first day of January, reading just two pages of the Book of Mormon each day, by the time September came you would have finished the entire book. Then, once you had finished with the book, you could start over and thus continue to "feast upon the words of Christ," as we are repeatedly commanded (see 2 Nephi 31:20; 32:3).

Reading and meditating on the words of Christ, we draw nearer to the Spirit. Once in tune, we can receive additional inspiration that will help guide our lives. Often the things we read on any given day will help us in one way or another before that day ends. As we are counseled in the Primary hymn, if we "search, ponder, and pray . . . the Spirit will guide, and, deep inside, [we'll] know the scriptures are true" (*Children's Songbook,* p. 109).

If you don't think you can arrange time sufficient to read two pages per day, do as a friend of mine has suggested: read for fifteen seconds, at least. Our chances for increasing spirituality in our lives are greatly enhanced when we come into contact with the inspired words of scripture. Every decision of our lives could be more inspired if we were to do this regularly.

Next, resolve to really pray, not just to say prayers. There is a big difference. Learn to pour out the real, in-depth feelings of your heart to Heavenly Father, rather than merely going through the form of prayer, using the same trite words and phrases every time.

I remember the experience of one bright missionary who came to the Missionary Training Center to begin learning Spanish. He had one major problem: He could not trill an *r.* His tongue didn't work that way. And you can't learn to pronounce Spanish well without trilling *r*'s. He worked, struggled, and prayed. A week before leaving the MTC, he had finally conquered his problem and triumphantly wrote a letter to his parents, the entire first page of which was filled with nothing but *r*'s. He later said that if he had not learned another thing in his entire mission than to humble himself and learn how to *really* pray, the whole experience would have been worth it.

Finally, "Remember the sabbath day, to keep it holy" (Exodus 20:8). The scriptures instruct us: "Six days shalt thou labour, and do all thy work: But the seventh day is the sabbath of the Lord thy God: in it thou shalt not do any work" (Exodus 20:9–10).

I had a personal experience in this area that changed my life for the better. It happened soon after I returned from my mission. I was enrolled at Brigham Young University, and the study requirements seemed to me to be extremely stringent. I had an advanced course with a very demanding professor, and every Monday morning we had a detailed examination on the assigned material. The competition was keen and I was highly motivated to do well.

I developed a habit of studying on Sunday afternoons, after attending regular church meetings, in preparation for what I knew would come on Monday mornings. On one of those afternoons, another returned missionary roommate observed what I was doing. He said, "Say, Joe, are you a Mormon? Do you *really* believe in keeping the commandments?" My answer was obvious: "Sure." "Then how about, 'Six days shalt thou labour, and do *all* thy work'?"

I got the message, and from that time on I changed my ways. I began to do a better job of organizing my study time during the other six days of the week. Occasionally, I found that I needed to get up early—and I mean *very* early—on Monday mornings to finish my preparation. But it worked, and continued working all through graduate school. I found that I procrastinated less—I knew I would have to get my studying done during the week. I couldn't let myself get behind. I felt better about myself and even noticed that my grades improved. As the saying goes, "Start early and finish happy." I began to look forward to the change of pace that Sunday provided, and took time to turn to things that were more spiritual.

I agree that there is some essential work that must be done on the Sabbath, and *occasionally* the ox does get in the mire for almost everyone. But usually, through poor organization or procrastination, we give the ox a little nudge.

Temptations to break the Sabbath are even greater now than they used to be. Television is a challenge. I love football, basketball—just about any athletic event. It doesn't matter who is playing. Barbara said to me once: "Joe, I don't understand you. It doesn't matter who is playing— Mars could be playing Jupiter and I'll bet you would be interested." I agreed that if Mars were playing Jupiter, I would *really* be interested.

As you know, some of the best games are televised on Sunday. Super Bowl or not, the temptation is great. Many Saints seem to justify regularly spending hours on Sunday in front of the tube watching the plays, replays, and almost endless post-game commentaries. Others, for whom sports may not be a temptation, often watch other programs on Sunday that are anything but spiritually uplifting.

I have discovered a wonderful advantage of technology: we simply use the VCR to record the Sunday programs we don't want to miss, and then on another day, at our own convenience, we can watch those special events—fast-forwarding through the commercials and time-outs. We don't have to miss a thing.

After we have attended our meetings and fulfilled our other Church duties, we don't have to sit and fold our hands on Sunday. There are many things we can do to make the day special. The following list of suggestions is based on counsel from President Spencer W. Kimball:

1. Set aside time for meditation.

2. Plan service to others.

3. Read the scriptures, conference reports, and Church publications.

4. Study the lives and teachings of the prophets.

5. Prepare Church lessons and other Church assignments.

6. Write to or visit relatives and friends.

7. Write to missionaries.

8. Enjoy uplifting music.

9. Read with a child.

10. Do family history research, or work on your personal history.

11. Sing Church hymns.

12. Read uplifting literature.

13. Develop an appreciation for the cultural arts.

14. Friendship nonmembers.

15. Visit the sick, the aged, and the lonely.

(See *Teachings of Spencer W. Kimball* [Salt Lake City: Bookcraft, 1982], p. 217.)

If we make Sundays special, then we can be helped to be more special in the sight of the Lord. It has been said, "It is not so much that the Jews kept the Sabbath, but rather, over the centuries, the Sabbath kept the Jews." Keeping the Lord's day holy can help keep us in the right way.

Reading scriptures regularly, praying more effectively, and keeping the Sabbath day holy are three sure ideas for increasing our spirituality. We can begin to implement them today, and will reap the benefits eternally.

Part Three: Summary

It will take energy and effort to keep all of our resolutions, but if we do, we will increase in wisdom, and in stature, and in favor with God and man (see Luke 2:52). By so doing, we will become a little more like the Savior every day for the rest of our lives. Each day will be better than the day before, and we will be more victorious over life's challenges. We will come to know more fully that Jesus is the Christ. He is our exemplar. He lives the way our Father in Heaven does, and we are commanded to become more like them.

In the short space of these few pages, obviously not everything could be included. You will undoubtedly have other good ideas geared to your personal situation, but a good foundation for resolutions can be built with these:

1. Resolve to expand your intellectual horizons.
2. Resolve to preserve and strengthen your physical body.
3. Resolve to be a truer friend.
4. Resolve to overcome inappropriate human pride.
5. Resolve to grow spiritually.

Now there is plenty of room for you to add to these your own suggestions about how to improve your marriage, your family, and yourself. The future strength of the Church, the community, and the world depends on how well we collectively do our part.

May we begin with ourselves by making resolutions that will assist us in increasing in wisdom, in stature, and in favor with God and man. If we do that personally, we will more nearly merit the blessings that come through a sound marriage relationship and a solid family. We will have done our part and we will be enabled to stand—and even kneel—with those who are dearest to us in the most sacred and holy of places: even the temple of our Lord.

All of this can be achieved in spite of what we see going on around us in a world experiencing increasing moral and spiritual pollution. To accomplish these ends will require our firmest resolutions—honestly made and genuinely kept. May that be our lot.

Index